PROJECT MANAGEMENT
IN LIBRARIES

ALA Editions purchases fund advocacy, awareness,
and accreditation programs for library professionals worldwide.

PROJECT MANAGEMENT IN LIBRARIES

On Time, On Budget, On Target

CARLY WIGGINS SEARCY

ALA Editions

CHICAGO 2018

CARLY WIGGINS SEARCY holds an MIS from the University of Michigan and has worked in public, special, and academic libraries for twenty years. She is a certified project management professional with experience that includes managing software development teams, implementing RFID systems, and surviving three library building projects. She currently lives in Louisiana, where she is the government information librarian for McNeese State University.

© 2018 by the American Library Association

Extensive effort has gone into ensuring the reliability of the information in this book; however, the publisher makes no warranty, express or implied, with respect to the material contained herein.

ISBN: 978-0-8389-1719-0 (paper)

Library of Congress Cataloging-in-Publication Data
Names: Searcy, Carly Wiggins, author.
Title: Project management in libraries : on time, on budget, on target / Carly Wiggins Searcy.
Description: Chicago : ALA Editions, an imprint of the American Library Association, 2018. | Includes bibliographical references and index.
Identifiers: LCCN 2018016386 | ISBN 9780838917190 (print : alk. paper)
Subjects: LCSH: Library administration. | Library planning. | Project management.
Classification: LCC Z678 .S43 2018 | DDC 025.1—dc23 LC record available at https://lccn.loc.gov/2018016386

Cover design by Karen Sheets de Gracia.

Text design in the Chaparral, Gotham, and Bell Gothic typefaces.

♾ This paper meets the requirements of ANSI/NISO Z39.48-1992 (Permanence of Paper).
Printed in the United States of America

22 21 20 19 18   5 4 3 2 1

Contents

Preface

LIBRARIANS MANAGE PROJECTS. INTRODUCING A NEW SUMMER reading program, updating library catalog software, and renovating a library building are all examples of typical library projects. Librarians work in a time of rapid social and technological change, and we have been implementing new and better products and services in response.

Much of the literature on project management is focused on for-profit endeavors. Companies use project management to protect profits and shield their investors from risk. *Profit* and *investors* are not words that resonate with library staff. *Services* are the focus of library work, and the word *patrons* honors the history of libraries as a shared investment. Sometimes the most passionate staff members are resistant to using business processes like project management in their unique library models. They argue that the mission and structure of libraries are radically different from that of corporations, and they are correct. In the corporate world, the more purchases of products and services, the more revenue for the company. Nonprofits don't make more with increased use, and in times of need, we're usually doing more with less.

I became a project manager out of necessity. I was managing a branch for a well-funded large public library when my family had to move for my husband's job. I left my beloved branch, colleagues, and community behind and moved to a rural area with few jobs. I was lucky to find a position in a school helping youth access college opportunities. Then I moved again, this time as a single mother with two children. I needed to take my seventeen years of experience in libraries and my information science degree and parlay them into meaningful, decent-paying work. After hundreds of applications, I got one interview for a job as a project manager for a nonprofit educational software development company. I reminded myself that I had managed projects in libraries and that I would figure out the rest. I made it through the interview, got the job, and got busy learning. Since then, I have worked on software development projects and earned my Project Management Professional (PMP) credential, and now I'm back home in the library, managing projects like data conversion and relocation.

I wish that I had known twenty years ago what I know now. I would have saved myself a lot of stress and frustration and saved my teams from rework and missed deadlines. With more knowledge about communication, scope, and change management, I would have been a more effective leader. I would have known how to make sure projects stayed within budget, finished on time, and achieved the strategic goals of the library.

While I value my PMP credential, that in-depth knowledge isn't necessary for most library professionals. Most library professionals need practical strategies, tools, and tips to address the specific challenges of project work in libraries. *Project Management in Libraries* will help library leaders who are managing projects to thrive, not just survive.

Acknowledgments

W E ACCOMPLISH LITTLE IN PROJECTS AND IN LIFE ALL BY ourselves.

Lisa Armato and the rest of the awesome staff at Allen County Public Library in Indiana taught me how to manage libraries. Don Dailey at Kalamazoo Regional Educational Services Agency took a chance and hired a librarian to be a project manager and then hired me again to be a data coordinator. Working with the crew at the Learning Network of Greater Kalamazoo and our community partners was the toughest job I ever loved.

Thanks to my colleagues at McNeese State University for welcoming me to Louisiana and for sharing both a move project *and* an RFID project with me. I'd also like to thank the members of the Library Think Tank group on Facebook who took the time to share their interests in project management with me. Finally, thanks to my family, who has always encouraged me to do things I didn't think I could do, like earning my PMP credential and writing a book. It's good to have a team.

1

The Basics

IT'S EASY TO THINK OF MUCH OF THE WORK IN LIBRARIES AND life as projects. People use the word *project* almost like *chore*: "It was a major project just getting out of my house this morning!"

In project management, there is a distinction between the ordinary operations of the organization and projects. The regular, everyday work of the organization (that follows existing procedures) falls under operations. Limited endeavors that create a unique product or service are projects.

I was once part of a facilities enhancement for a public library system that built a few new branches, renovated several branches, and added on to the main library. This work lasted about five years. During that time, we continued to do the regular business of a library as well—materials selection, reference, circulation, and programming. Were the facilities improvements a project? Remember, the essential characteristics of a project are a limited time frame and a unique result. Our renovations had a beginning and an end. The renovations created a unique product or service. In fact, each building was unique and had a start and end date for construction. The work done at each location was an individual project.

Library programs that happen every week are not projects, but creating and implementing the library's first online summer reading program *is* a project. Issuing payroll each month is not a project, but getting a bond passed to increase library revenue *is* a project.

REVIEWING MANAGEMENT

I worked as a library manager for many years before I took a management class and learned the official definition of the term *management*. Management is "the process of using organizational resources to achieve organizational objectives through planning, organizing, and staffing, leading and controlling."[1]

PUTTING IT TOGETHER
A Definition of Project Management

If management is using resources to achieve objectives and a project is a limited endeavor to create a unique product or service, then project management must be *the use of organizational resources to create a unique product or service that achieves organizational objectives.* The official definition of project management from the Project Management Institute (PMI) is "the application of knowledge, skills, tools, and techniques to project activities to meet the project requirements."[2]

THE PROJECT MANAGEMENT INSTITUTE

PMI is a globally recognized body that establishes project management knowledge and certification. It is a nonprofit organization and does some of the same things that ALA does for the profession of librarianship. PMI is responsible for accreditation, standards, research, publications, and professional development. PMI also offers credentials and certification for project managers. For example, PMI issues the Project Management Professional (PMP) credential.

WHY PROJECT MANAGEMENT MATTERS

Why invest time reading a book about project management? In 2016, only 53 percent of projects were completed within the original budget, and only 49 percent of projects were completed on time.[3] In fact, the larger the project, the higher the chance of failure: large projects have twice the chance of being late, being over budget, and missing critical features than smaller projects.[4] Libraries cannot afford to spend time and money on projects that fail to meet their goals. It is our commitment to utilize limited resources for the greatest good that makes project management such a good fit for libraries. We have a mission to carry out, and we take our responsibility seriously.

I have invested my time in learning project management because I believe it creates better outcomes for those we serve. Early in my career, I did not enjoy thinking about library business processes, efficiency, or funding. I loved executing the daily business of a library. I enjoyed programming and getting children excited about reading and learning. I liked my shifts at the information desk, providing reference and readers' advisory services. I had the best job in the world. Then I watched as my library and many others lost significant amounts of revenue. We struggled to meet increased demand for services with less staff. I was frustrated by the changes but unsure how I could address them. I felt like an observer rather than a participant. I moved to the field of education and saw more of the same: public servants struggling to help their communities despite radical cuts to funding. I'm not a proponent of doing more with less, and I won't try to sell that package of goods. I am a proponent of figuring out what matters and doing it well. Employing project management techniques helps organizations use their resources to do the most good.

In the last few years, I've started to see job postings for library project managers. Project management is a competency for information professionals by the Library Leadership and Management Association (LLAMA), Special Libraries Association (SLA), and the Library of Congress. LLAMA, WebJunction, and state library agencies have all offered project management webinars. Library leaders see project management as a valuable skill set as libraries adapt to technological and social changes. Jane Kinkus noted, "Not only does the progression of technology seem to be introducing more opportunities for project-based work in libraries, but the increased complexity caused by a project's need for expertise from multiple departments leads to an increased need for project management skills in modern librarian jobs."[5] Project management skills can help you thrive in the job that you have and increase your marketability for the future.

WHAT PROJECT MANAGERS DO

Doing project management means using a systematic method to plan and complete projects successfully.

The project manager is the person focused on project success. He or she should have the authority to assign resources (like people) and to spend money allocated to the project to achieve the project's goals. Sometimes library staff members are asked to manage projects without being given the power to spend money. While officially that difference changes the role of project manager to project coordinator, your organization may not recognize this distinction. Many unofficial project managers in libraries are held responsible for the success of the project but don't have the authority to assign resources or spend money. Understanding this distinction could be helpful in making a case for more authority or less responsibility.

Project managers manage the process and people. Because people do the work of projects, project management is both a science and an art. Depending on their strengths, managers tend to focus on either the process or the people. Most of us like doing what we are good at—and avoid what is challenging or new. Using project management techniques means focusing on both elements. That is the recipe for project success.

HOW TO USE THIS BOOK

This book focuses on practical project management. It will not cover all forty-seven project management processes or every tool, technique, and output in PMI's formal project management methodology. That would be overwhelming and more than most library projects require.

PMI's model does not teach project management as a sequence of events because projects are iterative. Sometimes a piece of information required to complete a step just isn't there, and the team must forge ahead until it becomes available. Things change over the course of a project, and sometimes the team will revisit a decision or a plan and make modifications. I have attempted to put the essential processes of project management in sequential order to give an overview of the entire process from start to finish. You will adjust the sequence of events to fit your unique project needs.

You will also modify the steps in this book to match the resources and scale of your project. Small projects require less project management. You can condense your plans down to a page or two for a small project.

The focus of this book is not on earning a PMP credential but on building knowledge and skills and using tools and techniques for better project management in libraries. For those who want to learn more about formal project management, the section "About PMI Certification" at the end of this chapter provides an overview of the process.

UNDERSTANDING THE FIVE PROCESS GROUPS

Every project should go through five phases. The phases, called "process groups," are initiating, planning, executing, monitoring and controlling, and closing. These phases are helpful for dividing your work and concentrating on specific actions for each process. The process groups can keep a complex project from being overwhelming. Even on small projects, the five phases help organize work and ensure that critical steps get completed before moving forward. The next several chapters in this book are arranged around the five process groups, beginning with initiating.

Figure 1.1 shows a high-level view of the flow through the process groups. Specific things happen in each phase of the project.

- In initiating, we gather preliminary information and formally commit to the project.
- In planning, we decide how we will accomplish the project.
- In executing, people do the work of the project.
- In monitoring and controlling, we make sure we achieve the objectives of the project.
- In closing, we get formal acceptance that the project is complete.

These phases aren't unique to project management—I move through them every time I plan a meal. When I get home from work, I decide whether or not to have dinner. I *initiate* dinner. Next, I talk with my team (my husband, son, and daughter) to *plan* whether we're going to cook or get takeout. Once those decisions are made, we *execute*. My husband chops the onion while I smash the

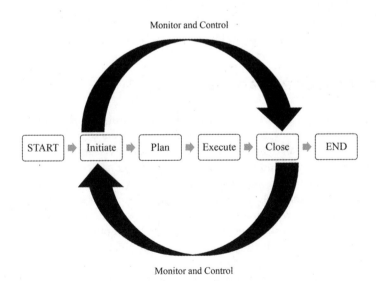

FIGURE 1.1
Project Management Process Groups

garlic and turn on the frying pan. While we are executing, we *monitor* the oil in the pan so it doesn't smoke, and we *control* the flame. When everyone has eaten, we *close*: we sit around the table and discuss what we liked and how to make the dish better next time.

In Figure 1.1, you will notice that monitoring and controlling happens simultaneously with all the other phases of the project. Monitoring and controlling help us to spot problems and resolve them as early as possible. When I get my hair cut, if the stylist starts cutting off inches and I didn't ask for that, I don't wait until "closing" to say something. I monitor what's happening, and I speak up right away when I have a concern.

In an ideal world, we would plan a project, and it would be carried out just as expected. That never happens. We make decisions in one phase of the project that we revisit when we get to the next phase, responding to new information, adding detail, and making sure that we don't get derailed by change requests. Expect challenges, plan to gather information throughout the project, and be ready to revisit every part of your plan. Project management is not linear—there are feedback loops throughout the process. Continuously improving and detailing the plan as you go—as more information becomes available—is called *progressive elaboration*.

Project management doesn't keep us from making mistakes—it gives us a process to catch issues early and respond to them. If your project has never been done before, you and your team will make mistakes, learn from them, and make adjustments. The more unique and complex the project, the more you will "fail forward." Each step in the process group phases is designed to minimize the impact of the things you didn't know, the things you didn't expect, and the things you didn't want to happen.

AGILE PROJECT MANAGEMENT

If you're interested in project management, you have probably heard of Agile. It was created in 2001 by a group of software developers who called themselves "organizational anarchists." Like any revolution, it was informed by previous paradigm shifts, including Deming's total quality management and lean manufacturing principles developed in Japan.

Agile sounds deceptively simple. For example, one of the twelve principles is "At regular intervals, the team reflects on how to become more effective, then tunes and adjusts its behavior accordingly." In practice, this means changing old habits in both thinking and behavior. That simple principle is hard work.

Agile project management requires specific conditions to be successful, and it requires dedication to learn and implement this formal methodology.

It's rigorous. For this reason, most organizations use a hybrid approach to project management—they use both Agile and traditional methods.

This book won't teach you Agile project management. Instead, I'll introduce a few ideas borrowed from Agile practice that I've used in projects. I have sprinkled three Agile project management practices throughout the book: self-organizing teams, rolling wave planning, and short daily meetings. If you're interested in Agile, try out these ideas and see if they work for your team.

ABOUT PMI CERTIFICATION

Projects are a lot of hard work. Why would you want to earn a professional project management certification and do more? A professional certification might be the right fit for you if you meet the following criteria:

- You love managing process, people, and projects.
- You want to switch careers.
- You need a credential to move up.
- You want to earn more (and are willing to leave libraries if necessary).

Earning a project management credential is going to cost you time and money. How much depends on which certification you pursue. For beginners, PMI offers the Certified Associate in Project Management (CAPM). They also offer the Project Management Professional (PMP) for those with more experience managing projects. If you love Agile concepts, the Scrum Alliance offers the Certified Scrum Master (CSM) credential. None of these are inexpensive or quick, so I recommend you do additional research before you choose.

The PMP certification from PMI is the credential I chose to pursue. I had the required years of work experience as a dedicated project manager, and I knew I could earn the thirty-five class hours in a reasonable time frame. If you are interested in the PMP certification, there are a few things you should know. There is no specific roadmap for preparation. There are an abundance of choices to make, from the coursework you take to the way you study for the test.

There are hundreds of education providers who offer courses of varying formats. You can take a week-long boot camp that meets face-to-face or a semester-long online course. Whatever format you choose, the provider must be certified through PMI as a "registered education provider." That list is available on the PMI website. Before investing in any courses, find out what the pass rate on the exam is for their students. Don't pay $5,000 for boot camp if only 50 percent of students pass the test on their first try. I took four online courses from a registered provider at a fraction of the cost of a boot camp. I don't know if a boot camp would have better prepared me for the test, but I definitely saved money.

Once you have the required thirty-five class hours, you are ready to complete the application to sit for the PMP test. That application requires you to provide in-depth information about your previous project management experience. I recommend you make a spreadsheet of your experience before you attempt to fill out the application. Some applicants get "audited," and the spreadsheet will be your documentation of the hours you reported. I was not audited, was accepted to take the exam, and registered for a date three months out. The test currently costs $555 if you are not a member of PMI or $405 if you are a member. PMI membership is $139, so you can save a few dollars by joining the organization first and then registering.

The test is designed to measure the application of knowledge, and that means that there aren't specific questions and answers to study. I selected a PMP study guide as thick as a phone book. I developed a schedule for reading that included getting up at 4:30 each morning. When I began preparing for my PMP exam, I would say, "I'm preparing to take the exam." After a few months of study, I switched to saying, "I'm preparing to pass the exam." I identified my strengths and weaknesses. I used short breaks in my day to furiously write out the formulas and the forty-seven processes that I would use as my reference material for the test. As my test date approached, I took a few sample tests and decided I was not yet ready. I changed my test date (which cost $100) to give myself another month to study.

The test is two hundred questions to be answered within four hours. Taking the test was mentally exhausting. Most of the questions are complex and have more than one right answer. Even with all my preparation, midway through the test, I started to doubt that I was going to be successful. I reminded myself that I had not invested my time and money to fail. I straightened my shoulders and kept going. When I finished the test, I clicked and waited for my results to appear on screen and...I passed!

The test was a reminder for me that commitment, a plan, hard work, and determination are still the ingredients in any recipe for success. I invested months of my free time and a significant amount of money. In exchange, I was no longer an accidental project manager; I became an intentional project manager.

My total cost, including membership to PMI, classes, the test, and materials, was just over $2,000. That's about as cheaply as it can be done. The cost of obtaining the Certified Scrum Master (CSM) credential is similar to the PMP. If Scrum is a better fit for your style, the types of projects you do, or your industry, you may find you can earn that credential faster than the PMP.

SUMMING UP

- [ ] Make sure your projects are *actually* projects. If a project doesn't create a unique product or service *or* it never ends, it's not a project.
- [ ] Project management is all about iterations. Expect to revisit decisions and to revise plans throughout the project.
- [ ] If you're an accidental or unofficial project manager, you may not have the authority to assign resources or spend money. If that's the case, have a conversation with your sponsor to clarify who is responsible for project success.

NOTES

1. Andrew J. DuBrin, *Essentials of Management*, 9th ed. (Mason, OH: South-Western / Thomson Learning, 2012).
2. Project Management Institute, *A Guide to the Project Management Body of Knowledge: PMBOK® Guide* (Newtown Square, PA: Project Management Institute, 2017).
3. Project Management Institute, "The High Cost of Low Performance," *PMI's Pulse of the Profession*, 2016, www.pmi.org/-/media/pmi/documents/public/pdf/learning/thought-leadership/pulse/pulse-of-the-profession-2016.pdf.
4. Michael Webber and Larry Webber, *IT Governance: Policies and Procedures* (Alphen aan den Rijn, Netherlands: Wolters Kluwer Law & Business, 2016).
5. Jane Kinkus, "Project Management Skills: A Literature Review and Content Analysis of Librarian Position Announcements," *College and Research Libraries* 68, no. 4 (2007): 352–63, http://crl.acrl.org/index.php/crl/article/download/15880/17326.

2
Characteristics of a
Project Manager

The achievement of difficult goals requires...the sustained
and focused application of talent over time.

—J. B. Connell, *Flying without a Helicopter*

JENNIFER IS A YOUNG ADULT LIBRARIAN WORKING IN HER
first professional position at a public library. Because she did some web
development work in graduate school, Jennifer is asked to lead a committee charged with redesigning the library's website. Though she has concerns
about managing a project of this size, Jennifer agrees immediately. She knows
this is a career-building opportunity.

When she starts to plan the first committee meeting, it dawns on Jennifer that she doesn't know where to begin. She vaguely remembers a session
at her state library conference on project management and decides to refresh
her memory. Jennifer checks out a book on project management to read
over the weekend. She learns the formal definition of a project and is sure
website redesign fits the bill. Jennifer reads about the five stages of project

management and decides those make a lot of sense. Next, she learns there are ten knowledge areas, and some of the language is unfamiliar. *Stakeholders*, *procurement*, *integration*, and *scope* are new terms. She starts to wonder if project management will be a fit for her project. Finally, Jennifer turns the page to a chart listing forty-seven project management processes. Forty-seven. She wants to throw the book at the wall.

After her frustration passes, Jennifer considers that the project management model does provide an abundance of direction. She knows that she needs a map to lead this committee through this project. Jennifer returns to her book. She may have been appointed committee chair, but Jennifer decides she's also going to be the project manager and work through the steps together with her planning committee.

I hope to spare you Jennifer's frustration by giving you a lighter version of the forty-seven project management processes. No matter what framework you have, though, doing things in new ways will get messy. It is a law of nature that things fall apart. Your job is to minimize the mess and bring order where you can. The project manager occupies a unique leadership position, requiring specific traits and qualities. You will need an abundance of persistence. You will need to work effectively with people who have different personalities, work styles, and priorities. All the while, you will need to treat everyone with respect and fairness. In this chapter, I highlight a few characteristics worth cultivating.

BE TENACIOUS

Roy Tennant said that "the single best tech skill is tenacity," and that's true in project management as well.[1] The most important skill a project manager needs is the ability to commit. Project management is a discipline. Maintaining fidelity to the model throughout the project is the only way to realize benefits from using project management practices.

Like many library project managers, Jennifer's authority is informal. She doesn't directly supervise the people appointed to her committee. As project manager, Jennifer will need to inspire people, but first, she needs her coworkers to trust her. One way project managers build trust is by doing what they say they will do. Day after day, Jennifer must pull it all together. She has to collaborate with people who may not agree on how to do the work, what the final product should look like, or when the project is complete. Jennifer must balance cost, time, quality, and risk. Tenacity is the skill Jennifer needs most, and the most significant investment she can make is with her energy.

A librarian friend of mine, Melissa Kiser, had a blog titled *The Finisher*. I've made this my project mantra: "In a world of starters, be a finisher." Being a finisher means getting and staying organized. Setting goals, providing regular communication, creating and updating plans and documents, and keeping deadlines are all basic project management tasks, each requiring a high level of organization. Take on only those commitments you can keep and then work diligently to complete them.

Tenacity alone makes an insufferable project manager. It does take some additional skills to be a competent leader. The good news is that many of the competencies required are the same as those necessary to be successful as a library professional. In both fields, success requires soft skills, like creativity and teamwork, in addition to subject matter knowledge and a strong will.

BE COLLABORATIVE

The rules for work are changing. We're being judged by a new yardstick—not just by how smart we are or by our training and expertise but also by how well we handle ourselves and each other.

DANIEL GOLEMAN
Working with Emotional Intelligence

Daniel Goleman's work on emotional intelligence is helpful for understanding the soft skills needed to lead projects successfully. He separates emotional intelligence into two broad categories: personal and social competences. Personal competence includes self-awareness, adaptability, and motivation. Social competence includes empathy and social skills.[2] Collaboration requires both types of competences.

Jennifer demonstrated several of these competences. She was self-aware enough to know that she needed help. She showed adaptability in her willingness to learn something new and motivation by carrying through reading even when the material got overwhelming. Leading a team will require empathy and social skills as well. Jennifer's future success will depend on her ability to engage her team in collaboration.

BE ETHICAL

Librarians are proud of our professional commitment to ethics such as intellectual freedom and each library user's right to privacy. Tough decisions are made easier because of those principles. Our ALA Code of Ethics simplifies working with library colleagues because we can assume we share foundational values. I was surprised to learn that project managers have a robust code of ethics as well. Working in nonprofits for so long, I had become cynical about the business sphere—where project management was born.

Just as ALA provides our code of ethics, the Project Management Institute (PMI) provides a "Code of Ethics and Professional Conduct" for professional project managers.[3] Some elements in the code are aspirational, while others are mandatory. For instance, project managers aspire to take responsibility for their decisions, but reporting illegal conduct is mandatory. The core values of the project management code of ethics are responsibility, respect, fairness, and honesty. Those four values will appear throughout this book.

While I've prepared myself for the FBI to come into the library and request circulation records that show who has checked out *The Anarchist's Cookbook*, my actual ethical dilemmas in libraries have never been quite that dramatic. Similarly, as a project manager, no vendor has offered me a bag of cash to award a contract to them. My ethical challenges have always been more subtle and usually involved a choice between ignoring a problem and doing something difficult but honest and necessary.

We all think of ourselves as honest. Sometimes an ethical dilemma arises when we have to choose between honesty and protecting people we like and respect. The person we want to protect might even be ourselves. I was implementing a new software system across several organizations. The team hosted a big training event to show staff how to enter data. We created training materials, videos, and documentation and posted them online for staff to reference as needed. A few weeks after the event, it was clear that some users were struggling. In some locations, the Internet connection was a problem. In others, computers were too old to handle the demands of the new system. In some organizations, staff members were skilled at working with people and not skilled at working with data. We worked hard over the following months to solve the connection and hardware issues and to retrain staff. Then our first reporting cycle came along, and when we exported our data, it was clear that one location had incomplete, inconsistent, and inaccurate data. Reporting the data could negatively impact individuals and the team, including the possibility of losing funding. As the project manager, I worried that the situation would reflect negatively on me as well.

PMI's code of ethics is clear. It states that project managers will provide accurate information promptly. While my impulse might have been to sugarcoat the interpretation of the data, as the project manager, it was my job to share accurate information so that we could address the issues together. If we could solve the problem at this location, we would better understand how to support additional organizations as they joined the group. I knew I needed to report the data in our written report. I made a heads-up phone call to the team leader, gave her a summary of the report, and assured her we would work together on a solution. Then I released the report and scheduled a follow-up meeting. I could have quietly released the report and fulfilled my obligation for honesty, but that would have been poor leadership. I would have overlooked the additional ethical values of respect and responsibility. I was obligated to share the data, and I had an opportunity to work with the team and build trust. Both were critical to the long-term success of the project.

In my experience, ALA's Code of Ethics and PMI's Code of Ethics are mutually reinforcing. The ALA Code reads, "We protect each library user's right to privacy and confidentiality."[4] The PMI Code states, "We protect proprietary or confidential information that has been entrusted to us."[5] If in doubt, I choose the statement that places a more substantial burden on me to act ethically.

AN ETHICAL DECISION-MAKING FRAMEWORK

It's easy to say "Be ethical," but complex dilemmas sometimes require us to balance competing needs and desires. In those situations, PMI's ethical decision-making framework may be helpful.[6] The five steps are assessment, alternatives, analysis, application, and action:

1. **Assessment:** Do I have all the information?
2. **Alternatives:** What are my options?
3. **Analysis:** What will be the impact of each choice on everyone involved?
4. **Application:** Does my proposed solution conflict with the code of ethics?
5. **Action:** Which decision am I willing to accept public responsibility for making?

Committing to working through these steps ensures that all options are considered. An additional benefit I discovered is that using the framework buys time needed for rational thinking. A library director once told me, "I need you to speed this data conversion up and finish one month earlier than planned." I did not think we could accomplish our work a month ahead of the plan with existing resources. I answered honestly, "I don't know if that's possible. I need a day to research our options." With that answer, I bought myself some time. I was able to get out of the emotionally charged situation of thinking *We're already working so hard. Why does he make these unreasonable demands? How am I supposed to tell the director no?* Instead, I used the five steps to list and analyze my options.

First, I assessed the situation. I knew the staff well. I had data on the amount of work the group could accomplish in a single day. I didn't think they could work faster.

Second, I considered three alternatives. We could continue as planned. Another option would be running parts of our project at the same time that we had intended to do sequentially. Finally, we could add resources.

I analyzed each option, considering the impact on everyone involved. We could stick to our original timeline. That would delay our launch and negatively impact our library users. Running parts of the project at the same time was not going to help because we were already doing that where possible. Adding resources was looking like the best option.

I checked my possible solution, asking staff to work more hours on the project, against the code of ethics. I saw two standards to uphold, respect and fairness. First, we could not respectfully ask staff to work without compensation. Second, the opportunity to work extra hours should be offered to all qualified candidates to be fair.

When I went back to the director with my proposed action, I had an answer I was confident in giving. I was able to say, "Yes, we can be done a month earlier if I can offer compensatory time to our staff." My initial impulse to answer "No, because..." was replaced with "Yes, if..." That's a much stronger position for any project manager.

Many of us instinctively do some of the five steps in the framework when facing any challenge. The problem is that we tend to focus on the steps where we have experience or that use our natural talents. We often skip the steps that are most challenging. Using the framework ensures we don't miss a step.

SUMMING UP

- ☐ Project managers must practice responsibility, respect, fairness, and honesty.
- ☐ Most of us are naturally skilled at tenacity or emotional intelligence, not both. Identify which of these is a weakness for you. Consider ways you could build your competence in that area.
- ☐ Use project management tools like the ethical decision-making framework to give yourself time to consider all options before you answer a request.

NOTES

1. Roy Tennant, "The Single Best Tech Skill Is Tenacity," The Digital Shift, posted January 25, 2012, www.thedigitalshift.com/2012/01/roy-tennant-digital-libraries/the-single-best-tech-skill-is-tenacity/#_.
2. Daniel Goleman, *Working with Emotional Intelligence* (New York: Bantam Books, 2006).

3. Project Management Institute, "Code of Ethics and Professional Conduct," last revised October 2006, www.pmi.org/-/media/pmi/documents/public/pdf/ethics/pmi-code-of-ethics.pdf?sc_lang_temp=en.

4. American Library Association, "Professional Ethics," last revised January 22, 2008, www.ala.org/tools/ethics.

5. Project Management Institute, "Code of Ethics and Professional Conduct."

6. Project Management Institute, "Ethical Decision-Making Framework," 2012, www.pmi.org/-/media/pmi/documents/public/pdf/ethics/ethical -decision-making-framework.pdf?sc_lang_temp=en.

3
Meeting Management 101

PROJECT MANAGERS ACCOMPLISH THEIR WORK THROUGH other people, and people plan their work together in meetings. Face-to-face meetings are an opportunity to brainstorm, to have meaningful conversations, and to reach collective decisions. As the project manager, you are essentially asking people over and over again, "Will you help me solve this?" You will use meetings to engage team members and get feedback, insight, and commitment from the people who are going to do the work of the project.

In 2014, the consulting firm Bain & Company estimated that 15 percent of an organization's time is spent in meetings. That number has continued to increase each year since 2008.[1] Poorly run meetings are one of the most significant time sinks in the workplace. I once attended a meeting that lasted three hours and ended with no decisions made, no action items assigned, and no follow-up. I left frustrated, thinking of all the work I could have completed during those three hours.

Running effective meetings is a skill that can be learned, and it is one every project manager needs. A productive meeting requires advanced preparation, skilled facilitation, and a meaningful conclusion. The checklist in Figure 3.1 will help you hit the finer points in these three areas.

✓	**ADVANCED PREPARATION**
	Before the Meeting
	1. Define the purpose of the meeting.
	2. Create a meeting agenda.
	a. Review action items from the last meeting.
	b. Ask key stakeholders for input as needed.
	3. Determine how much time you will need.
	4. Identify technology needs.
	5. Scout locations and choose one.
	6. Find date and time.
	7. Communicate details to participants.
	a. Send meeting invite with plenty of notice.
	b. Include agenda.
	c. Send additional documents.
	d. Ask for review, feedback, or additions.
	e. Add link to a survey if needed.
	8. Make calls to those with items on the agenda and new members.
	9. Prewire your meeting.
	10. Order food/beverages.
	11. Print your slides and have presentation on flash drive and in e-mail.
	Set Up the Meeting
	1. Identify bathroom location.
	2. Bring materials.
	3. Pull up slides and websites before the meeting.
	4. Set up food and water.
	5. Put up any signage needed.
	6. Display agenda on screen or make copies available. (Do you need large print?)
✓	**SKILLED FACILITATION**
	Start the Meeting
	1. Mention location of bathrooms.
	2. Share meeting norms.
	3. Tell the group you will use a "parking lot" as a way to document items that are important but outside the scope of the meeting. Make this list visible to the group (I use big sticky paper on the wall).
	4. Introduce those taking notes, timekeeping, facilitating, and so forth.

	During the Meeting	
	1.	Take your own notes as needed.
	2.	Offer the group a break during meetings that last an hour or more.
✓	**MEANINGFUL CONCLUSION**	
	End the Meeting	
	1.	Finish on time.
	2.	Review action items and next steps.
	3.	Announce when notes will be sent.
	After the Meeting	
	1.	Send meeting notes with action items, parking lot items, and next steps.
	2.	Give credit and thanks.
	3.	Make individual follow-up calls as needed.

FIGURE 3.1
Meeting Checklist

PREPARE

In preparing for a meeting, define the purpose of having it. Use verbs if possible. For example, say "Identify project risks and brainstorm possible solutions." Establishing a purpose can help the group avoid unnecessary meetings. If you find that the sole purpose is to share information, you may want to communicate via e-mail rather than a face-to-face meeting. The purpose will also help you decide who needs to be part of the conversation. Meetings are resource intensive, so only invite those who need to attend. Finally, add the purpose to the agenda so that attendees understand why they need to participate and can come prepared for discussion and decision-making.

Review notes from any previous meetings to create a first draft of the meeting agenda. Be sure to include time to follow up on action items from the last meeting. Reach out to key stakeholders for additional agenda items as needed. Use the drafted agenda to estimate the amount of time you will need to meet, and then schedule only that amount of time. A thirty-minute meeting with a focused agenda can be a welcome surprise for meeting-weary attendees.

Identify any technology or supplies needed for the meeting based on the agenda. If you need a projector or a high-quality microphone for people joining remotely, those needs may limit the places you can gather. Choose a location that will be a good fit for the meeting. I like to visit the room long before the meeting to think about how I want to arrange the space. If you want the group to brainstorm, tables you can move into a semicircle can be helpful. If you need a whiteboard or easel, make sure the room has one or arrange to bring one in.

Find a date and time for the meeting. You may need to send out a Doodle poll (www.doodle.com) if you don't have access to a shared calendar with your meeting attendees. Confirm that the staff you need to attend can make that date and time before you send an invitation to the group.

Once all those steps are complete, you're ready to send a meeting invitation. Make sure to give enough advanced notice of the meeting so that the folks you need can be there. Send the request with the agenda attached and include other documents that will be discussed, like your slide deck. Your meeting can start as soon as the invitation goes out by asking attendees to review and provide feedback, or you can just ask them to "be ready to discuss." If you want to get information from those who are less likely to speak up publicly, include a link to a survey.

There may be a few calls to make before the meeting. If you have action items from the last meeting, you might call those responsible for the items and confirm they are ready to report. It's courteous and limits surprises during the meeting. You may want to call any people joining the meeting for the first time and welcome them.

You can also "prewire" your meeting by reaching out to important stakeholders to get their thoughts ahead of time. Prewiring is especially helpful if you will be discussing sensitive topics that could derail the meeting. I was asked to facilitate a meeting with my boss's bosses on a sensitive topic. I wasn't aware of all the issues before the group or the personalities of the members, but my boss was. We created an agenda together and invited two other staff who knew the group members to role-play portions of the meeting. We "had it wired" by the time I got in front of my audience. We didn't do the work of the group—the decisions were theirs to make. We ensured that the decisions could take place by avoiding pitfalls during the meeting.

Arrange to provide beverages and food if possible. There is a lot of value in showing attendees that you've considered their needs and their comfort.

Print your materials and have them ready in digital form. If your technology fails, you'll want to have a backup solution. If you have a large group, a few copies of the agenda in large print are a thoughtful touch.

On the day of the meeting, schedule enough time to set up. Locate the bathrooms to prepare for that inevitable question. Put up any signage needed to help attendees locate the meeting. If you have handouts and a sign-in sheet, put those out. Set out food and water. Turn on any technology and open any files or websites you plan to use. Display the meeting agenda on screen if possible.

FACILITATE

Start all meetings by welcoming the group, introducing yourself, and restating the purpose of the meeting. Make time for people to introduce themselves if there are new members. Some facilitators like to use an icebreaker at this point. Icebreakers are simple games that get people talking and moving. Google "meeting icebreakers," and you will get a wealth of ideas that you can modify to suit your meeting.

If this is the group's first meeting, allow time to discuss norms or ground rules. You want group members to generate these, but you might need to get the discussion going by asking a question or two. Time, listening, confidentiality, decision-making, and participation are the areas that groups usually address with norms. You may want to ask about devices specifically. I prefer for meetings to be device-free, but that may not be possible. If the group does not suggest a norm around time, you may want to ask if they can agree to start on time and end on time. Bring the ground rules to each group meeting to post or mention briefly.

If you need a timekeeper, note taker, or someone to fill any other role, now is the time to ask the group to help. Sharing the work keeps group members involved and reinforces the idea that your meetings are not a time to rest. Be sure to switch up responsibilities from meeting to meeting.

Even if you have a scribe, you will want to jot down a few critical notes during the meeting. Use paper rather than your computer or phone so that attendees will see that your attention is on the meeting activities. Notes should include your action items; use them to keep yourself accountable for postmeeting follow-up.

Occasionally, meetings go awry, even with thoughtful preparation. There are some signs that a meeting isn't going well. If you see lots of side conversations, restlessness, and boredom, acknowledge this and ask if the group would like to take a break.

If you have a group where members are not speaking up, there are a few ways to invite participation. If the whole group is quiet, you might ask a question and go around the room, giving each attendee the opportunity to respond. You could pass out sticky notes and ask each person to write a quick response to a question and post it at the front of the room. Participants could form small groups to discuss an issue and then report back to the whole group. If you have individuals who are silent, invite "those who haven't spoken yet" to respond to an issue. Wait at least five seconds after you ask a question before you speak again. If you're stuck, you can simply ask the group why they're so quiet. Sometimes an honest question gets things moving.

If you have one group member who monopolizes the discussion, remind the group of their ground rules. If there isn't an applicable ground rule, acknowledge that you want to hear from more people.

If you have a serious issue in a meeting like two members arguing force-fully, share with the group what you are seeing. Ask them to help solve the problem. You might say, "I see that people are passionate about this subject. I want to make sure we use our time together wisely, and I'm concerned that we're not making progress toward our meeting's purpose. Is this something we should document and discuss outside this meeting?"

You can always end a meeting that's not productive. It demonstrates respect for everyone's time, and it allows you time to investigate the issue, address it in a smaller forum, and recover.

CONCLUDE THE MEETING

If you want attendees to be present and ready to start meetings on time, then you must give them the courtesy of ending meetings on time. If the meeting is going well but is in danger of running over time, ask the group if they want to keep going.

When you finish your agenda, end your meeting with a review of action items and next steps. You or your note taker will have been collecting them during the session. Let the group know when the meeting notes will be sent out.

Follow-up after the meeting is as important as having an agenda before the meeting. After the meeting, you have the opportunity to show attendees that you listened to them. Follow-up reinforces the idea that your meetings are worth attending. Send notes out as soon as possible after the meeting, ideally within a day. Those notes will include action items. In the e-mail, give credit to the group for their work. If there are individuals who contributed in significant ways, thank them in the e-mail or make a follow-up call.

SUMMING UP

- ☐ Identify a purpose for every meeting you hold, and make sure every invitee has a reason to attend.
- ☐ Use or adapt the meeting checklist to help you prepare, facilitate, and follow up on meetings.
- ☐ If a meeting isn't productive, end it.

NOTE

1. Bain & Company, "Busy CEOs Spend Nearly One Day Each Week Managing Communications, Two Days in Meetings," May 6, 2014, www.bain.com/about/press/press-releases/Busy-ceos-spend-nearly-one-day-each-week-managing-communications.aspx.

4
Find and Use the
Right Tool for the Job

DON'T YOU WISH THERE WAS A TOOL THAT YOU COULD BUY THAT would make managing projects easy? I do too. There are software tools that can help you manage projects, and it is just fun to choose software. However, new tools can also derail your project. New software can be expensive and time consuming. Your team could spend a lot of time choosing the software to use for managing the project, and your organization could spend lots of money to purchase it. The staff could invest lots of time learning the software. Choosing and implementing software could become a standalone project. For a large, multiyear project, that might be a good use of time and money. For smaller library projects, it is probably unnecessary. Finding the right tool for the job is essential. In some cases, the right tool is software you are already using.

I worked for a nonprofit that had a project management system, but it wasn't being utilized. When I asked about it, I was told, "It's not very good software." When I investigated, I found that projects had not been updated, files were organized inconsistently, and users simply gave up on it and eventually forgot their login credentials. When we invested in updating and reorganizing and then began using the system regularly to push information to stakeholders, it was worth it for our users to reset their credentials and start using the software.

If you think you may need a software purchase, start by assessing the tools you already have and that staff already know how to use. If you already have a tool that could work, use that. Next, consider your budget. If you don't have money, you'll need to use what you have or ask the project sponsor for funds. Figure 4.1, "Tools," provides a flowchart for decision-making based on your existing tools and your budget.

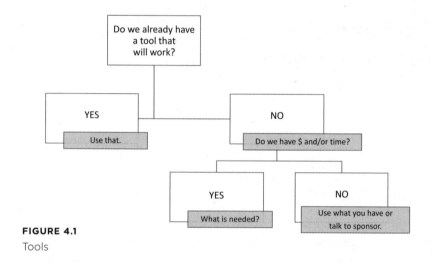

FIGURE 4.1

Tools

After answering these questions, if a software purchase is genuinely needed, you're ready to evaluate your needs, consider your options, and select, learn, and use the new tool.

EVALUATE YOUR NEEDS

1. What is it that you need that you don't have now? Is it organization, scheduling, time tracking, communication, task delegation, or something else?
2. What functionality does it need to have? Will you need to access remotely or via the web? Should it have reporting abilities? Will you use it to share private data and need a secure environment?

3. Who will use this tool? If you are not the only person who will use it, gather input from others. Think about who will access, who will edit, and who will manage the tool.

CONSIDER YOUR OPTIONS

Rank each software package you are considering. Ranking allows the group to give input and narrows the field to separate the needs from the wants. Ranking criteria could include the following:

1. **Functionality:** Does it do what you said you needed? If you need a hammer, don't buy a screwdriver because it might come in handy. Focus.
2. **Cost:** What will it cost (including licensing, training, maintenance, and customization)?
3. **Ease of use:** How easy will it be for people to learn? What kind of support will be needed?

LEARN IT AND USE IT

Your approach to learning will vary with the software package. If you selected a simple product that only the project manager will use, the help and support functions that are included might be enough. If more people will use the product, you may need to buy or create formal training. No software is so easy that it does all the work for you. While most software companies promise an easy-to-learn product with quick returns in efficiency, that's not been my experience. Typically, the more powerful the software, the more challenging it is to set up and use.

TYPES OF TOOLS

It's exciting to live in a time when there are options for almost every software need. The challenge is that choices are continually changing. Let's review a few options that are likely to remain available.

The Heavy Hitters: Microsoft Project, Oracle Primavera, and HP Project and Portfolio Management (PPM)

These are three expensive, powerful tools that have been around for years. They support rigorous traditional project management. These products really shine if your project is complex and you are going to make changes as you go along. Let's say you made a basic workflow and then created your schedules and budget based on that workflow. Later in the project, you need to make a change to the workflow. With this software, you can make one change to the workflow and have it cascade to the rest of your project documents.

Microsoft Project is by far the most affordable and the only one of the heavy hitters that is plug and play—you can use it out of the box. Different versions cost more or less depending on your needs. Project does a lot of the things that project management software should do—it handles scheduling, resources, and budgets. If you have a project plan and want to see what a particular change might do to your schedule, you can find out without recreating the wheel. It will take time to learn Project, though, even if you are the only one who will use it. Those working on smaller projects may spend more time learning the software than they save by using it.

The other two products, Oracle's Primavera and HP's PPM, require configuration. They also require multiple days of training and cost thousands of dollars. If you were building a new chemical plant or designing the next iPhone, these are the tools you would consider. Oracle's Primavera excels at project scheduling, and HP's PPM is especially useful for issue tracking. However, I can't recommend them for the vast majority of libraries and library projects because of their high cost and learning curves.

An Open Source Alternative: GanttProject

If you want the essential tools of Microsoft Project without the price tag, GanttProject is a good option. This free software can create charts to define and track work. Files can be imported from and exported to Microsoft Project, so it's a hit with Mac users. The interface is not intuitive, but resourceful learners can find plenty of tutorials online. It doesn't have all the bells and whistles of Project, but your project may not need them.

A Lightweight Alternative: Basecamp

If your needs are simple, Basecamp may be a good solution. It handles document management well and provides a secure environment for exchanging files containing sensitive data. It's great for organizing contacts for targeted communication. You can arrange contacts into multiple groups so that you send the right information to the right people. It is easy to use, and the customer support is excellent. Basecamp is an affordable choice with special pricing for nonprofits.

Two More Options: Trello and Asana

If you need to track tasks, both Trello and Asana are worth considering.

Trello is easy to use and is free or inexpensive, depending on your needs. It focuses on cards on boards to help you visualize project tasks at any moment. It's the more flexible of the two tools, allowing for a lot of customization. Trello provides for the creation of teams and team boards, making it useful for individuals or groups.

Asana also uses boards to organize tasks, is free or low cost, and works well for individuals or groups. Asana is more structured than Trello. If you don't want to do a lot of customization yourself, you may prefer Asana. Because you can sign up for free and both are relatively easy to learn and use, I recommend you test them both before making a decision.

By the time this book gets published, there will be new options in project management software, and some of the existing options may no longer be available. There are plenty of software reviews available to help you research your options. However, no software is going to solve all the challenges of project management for you.

SUMMING UP

- ☐ Unless you are working on a large project, the software that you already use may be the best tool for the job.
- ☐ Reach out to other libraries to ask about their experiences with software vendors and products.
- ☐ When evaluating the cost of software, be sure to include the costs of configuration, data conversion, staff training, documentation, and support.

5
Initiating

IN INITIATING, WE GATHER PRELIMINARY INFORMATION AND formally commit to the project. Initiating is the most romantic time in a project life cycle—it's when you get to think big about solving a problem. It's exciting to engage with leadership and consider building a new product or service. During initiating, three essential things happen. The project charter gets written, formal approval for the project gets secured, and all interested parties (stakeholders) get identified.

It's easy to jump right in with both feet and start planning a project. You may be confident you understand the project, have approval, and already know the stakeholders, but I've seen these assumptions get project managers in trouble. I've had a colleague refuse to share information because she hadn't been informed about her role in the project. I've worked with frustrated staff members who want to know why their organization is taking on this project at this time. I've seen extra work added to a project too many times to count. More time spent in initiating would have prevented all of these issues. As Sir John Harvey-Jones is reported to have said, "Planning is an unnatural process; it is much more fun to do something. The nicest thing about not planning is that failure comes as a complete surprise, rather than being preceded by a period of worry and depression."[1]

Time spent in initiating ensures that resources like time, energy, and money are spent well. In my library, money is in incredibly short supply. If we don't get it right the first time, we may not get a second chance. If the project is brief, inexpensive, and straightforward, the steps in initiating can be scaled back—but they should not be skipped. Time spent in initiating will pay dividends through the rest of the project.

WRITING THE CHARTER

A project charter is "a document...that formally authorizes the existence of a project and provides the project manager with the authority to apply organizational resources to project activities."[2]

When complete, the charter will be signed to authorize the project. It needs to tell the person signing it what the project is agreeing to do, so it should include a project purpose, objectives, requirements, assumptions and constraints, risks, milestones, and a budget. These elements provide the big picture of what needs to happen.

The project charter also tells everyone what is to be accomplished. Writing the charter forces you to quantify project objectives. If the goal is to move the library collection into a new building, one objective might be "Move 150,000 volumes from storage to the appropriate shelf locations in the renovated library by June 1." The charter clarifies the work of the project at a high level.

The information needed to write the charter comes from a few places—existing documents, environmental factors and organizational assets, expert judgment, and facilitation.

EXISTING DOCUMENTS

Documents are one source of information for writing the charter. I usually start here to build background knowledge. The library's strategic plan is a valuable reference document for drafting the charter. If the library put the project out for bid or is working with a vendor, the statement of work (SOW) for that contract will be helpful. Finally, previous project documents are another useful resource.

ENVIRONMENTAL FACTORS

I came to see, in my time at IBM, that culture isn't just one aspect of the game, it is the game. In the end, an organization is nothing more than the collective capacity of its people to create value.

—Louis Gerstner, IBM CEO and chairman of the board

Think back to the best place you've worked and the worst place you've worked. Was there a difference in the organizational culture between your two examples? Did the culture impact the work that you did? The saying "Culture eats strategy for lunch" reminds us that work on the project will happen within the workplace's existing environment.[3]

Environmental factors are "conditions not under the immediate control of the team that influence, constrain, or direct the project, program or portfolio."[4] Environmental factors can be internal or external to the organization and include the following:

1. **Organizational culture:** Library administration and staff may be change averse.
2. **Governmental regulations:** Your nonprofit status may restrict how you submit a project for bid.
3. **Market conditions:** Your library may be busier than ever due to an economic downturn and community job losses, or it may be less busy because your patrons are doing more research online at home.

All of these environmental factors shape the organization, the project, and the outcome of the project.

ORGANIZATIONAL ASSETS

Every library has assets that should be considered and used to benefit projects. Organizational assets are "plans, processes, policies, procedures, and knowledge bases that are specific to and used by the performing organization."[5] Assets include library policies, procedural manuals, templates, and stored information about previous projects. The collective knowledge of the people working on the project is another asset. Assets always help the project team do their work, while environmental factors may help or challenge the team.

Writing the charter also requires information that isn't in existing documents. Two tools will be used to fill in the gaps: expert judgment and facilitation techniques.

EXPERT JUDGMENT

Your facilities team would be consulted for a project to install a new HVAC system in the library. They are subject matter experts (SMEs) in facilities. If the library were installing a new conveyor system for book returns, circulation staff would serve as SMEs. Engaging SMEs as early as possible in the process is a smart move. SMEs challenge assumptions that you may not realize you are making. Working together sets up collaboration between departments early and builds a sense of shared ownership for the project.

FACILITATION TECHNIQUES

Brainstorming, conflict resolution, problem solving, and meeting management are four facilitation techniques used by project managers. All of these methods gather people together to share knowledge and create something new.

ROLES

At least one role is included in the charter: the sponsor. The sponsor is someone with power who will enable success. He or she is the critical person in writing the charter. The sponsor has the authority to commit resources to the project, and he or she will sign the completed charter. In an ideal world, the sponsor would write the charter. In most organizations, the project manager or other supporting staff member writes the charter under the sponsor's guidance. In addition to creating the charter and authorizing the project, the sponsor is the point of escalation for issues that go beyond the power of the project manager.

The charter often includes roles for staff in addition to the sponsor. The charter might also include the project manager, vendors, staff members, and board members to clarify who is responsible for what work.

OUTLINING THE EIGHT ELEMENTS OF A CHARTER

The elements that make up a project charter are the following:

1. Purpose
2. Objectives
3. Success criteria
4. Requirements

5. Constraints
6. Risk
7. Timeline
8. Cost estimates

Does this list seem like a daunting amount of information to gather at the start of a project? The process of creating the charter compels you to think through all that will be required to execute the project successfully.

PETE'S BIG PROJECT

Pete's library is getting renovated. Before renovation, the old security gates stopped functioning, and part of the renovation will include replacing the library security system. Pete's director let him know that she received a grant to implement radio frequency identification devices (RFID) for security. The director informs Pete that he is going to lead the project.

Pete knows that RFID implementation goes far beyond installing security gates—it requires every book to have an RFID tag inserted in it, for every tag to be encoded with the book's barcode number, and for staff to learn a whole new system for circulation. Pete has heard some horror stories from friends working in other libraries, and he's concerned about the size of this project. Pete decides that this project requires formal project management.

CHARTER ELEMENT #1: PURPOSE

Pete already knows the purpose of the project:

- The library will install an RFID system to replace the nonfunctioning security gates.

That's a start, but Pete adds some detail:

- University Library will be renovated from January 2016–July 2017. The renovation is an opportunity to replace obsolete equipment and increase efficiency.

Much better. Pete may have added a bit of work to the project with that "increase efficiency" line, but given the cost of RFID, the project does need to provide significant benefit. He takes another try:

- The thirty-year-old security gates are broken, and parts are no longer available. Also, the library has five fewer full-time staff members than it did two years ago. Radio frequency identification device (RFID) technology is the solution selected to replace the security system, to decrease staff workload via self-checkout, and to provide the additional benefit of inventory control.

Based on his knowledge and some organizational assets in the form of old e-mail messages and meeting notes, Pete has drafted a written project purpose. Pete's project sponsor is the library director. He should share this draft of the purpose with his director to ensure that his understanding matches hers.

CHARTER ELEMENT #2: OBJECTIVES

While Pete might be able to write the rest of the charter on his own, this is a good time for him to reach out to his coworkers. The objectives and requirements will be better if Pete writes them with input from others. Pete can reach out to stakeholders—his colleagues who also have a major stake in the project outcome.

Pete holds an informal meeting with a few subject matter experts from the staff. He chooses the head of circulation and a staff member from collection management. Before the meeting, Pete e-mails the drafted purpose statement (approved by the director) for his colleagues to review. Next, he drafts two objectives for the project. At the meeting, Pete begins by reviewing the purpose statement for the project. Next, he shares the draft of his two objectives:

1. All books will have an encoded RFID tag.
2. All RFID tags will be correctly encoded.

Pete asks for critical feedback. The head of circulation suggests an additional objective is needed to address the issue of efficiency:

1. Patrons will check out their books, freeing staff to complete other tasks.

CHARTER ELEMENT #3: SUCCESS CRITERIA

Next, Pete asks how the group will know if the project is successful. Together, they draft success criteria related to each objective.

1. All books will have an encoded RFID tag.

- **Success Criteria:** All 250,000 books in the general collection will be tagged and encoded by February 1, 2017.

2. All RFID tags will be correctly encoded.

- **Success Criteria:** Quality assurance will identify 5 percent or fewer errors with encoding.

3. Patrons will check out their books, freeing staff to complete other tasks.

- **Success Criteria:** Within two months, self-checkout will be used for 95 percent of all book loans.

By engaging his colleagues, Pete does more than get their feedback. He begins to see the project from their perspective. The meeting is on a roll, so Pete asks his colleagues if they can stay for another hour to discuss requirements, constraints, and risk.

CHARTER ELEMENT #4: REQUIREMENTS

Requirements are things that must be included in the results of the project. Requirements are often listed in any vendor contracts. If there is a contract, the project manager can pull those out and put them in the charter for easy reference. Pete and his colleagues identify two requirements for this project:

1. **Training for Staff:** Staff will require training on tagging and encoding books, assisting patrons with checkout, managing security, and inventory control. A portion of staff will require additional advanced training on software and system maintenance.
2. **Signage for Patrons:** Patrons will require clear, well-designed signage on how to use the new system for self-checkout.

Pete makes a note to check the vendor contract to make sure both requirements are included.

CHARTER ELEMENT #5: CONSTRAINTS

The charter outlines the feasibility of the project within limitations, also known as constraints. Time and cost are two constraints that library staff know well. The library has a limited budget to pay staff, so that's a cost constraint. Time is a constraint because the books must be tagged and encoded for the new library to open. Feasibility asks the question, "Can we deliver this project on time and within budget?"

The RFID group identifies two constraints:

1. **Number of Tags:** 286,000 tags are paid for, and 250,000 items are to be tagged. That leaves 36,000 additional tags for replacement, training, or new materials. If more than 36,000 additional tags are needed, additional funds will be required to purchase tags.
2. **Collections to Be Tagged:** Only the main collection will be RFID tagged. Items in local history and special collections will not be tagged.

CHARTER ELEMENT #6: RISK

All projects have risk, and the charter should identify high-level risks. Risks are events or conditions that can have a negative or positive effect on the project.

A risk in Pete's project is that they won't finish the project by the time the library renovation is complete. There are some ways the timeline could be negatively impacted, and the charter should identify that risk so that it can be further analyzed later. Positive risk is a little trickier to identify. Think of it as too much of a good thing. For example, a positive risk in Pete's project is that the renovated library will be so busy that more materials will circulate and there won't be enough stations to handle the higher use.

Pete's colleagues shared their worries that there wouldn't be enough staff to do the work, that the quality of the work might not be high enough, and that patrons might refuse to use the new system. They documented these risks in a list:

1. Staff will need to take on additional responsibilities during this project. Librarians and paraprofessionals must be available to work on this project at least ten hours per week to finish by July 2017. If a staff member resigns, is out sick, is unable to do the work, or is significantly slower than his or her peers, the timeline could be negatively impacted.
2. Quality of encoding tags must be high. If tags are not correctly encoded, staff will have to troubleshoot them at checkout, and that will result in no savings in time or even worse—it may take more time than the old system.
3. Patrons must utilize the new system to free staff to complete other tasks. If patrons do not use the new self-checkout system, there will be no savings in time.

Think of the risks outlined in the charter as a placeholder. If the project is approved, risks will be further analyzed.

CHARTER ELEMENT #7: TIMELINE

It makes sense to define the schedule in broad terms now so that the project sponsor can agree to the project's begin and end dates. At this stage, the timeline is a rough estimate.

There are a few options for estimating the timeline. You can do a top-down estimate, called apportioning. In apportioning, you assign estimates based on a percentage of the total. Instead of focusing on activities, you estimate portions of the entire project. If you know that training typically takes 15 percent of the time on a project, you can use that as an estimate. This method will work for the charter creation. Later in the project, more accurate methods will be used.

In Pete's case, the library has not done this type of project in the past, so he can't use other projects as the basis for his estimate. Instead, he uses the grant provided by the library director and the date of the library's reopening to create a simple timeline with a begin date, a few milestones, and an end date that is before the library reopens:

March 1, 2016: All equipment and tags received

April 1, 2016: Core staff trained by vendor

May 1, 2016: All library staff trained

September 1, 2016: All reference books encoded with less than 5 percent error rate

February 1, 2017: All 250,000 items encoded with less than 5 percent error rate

March 1, 2017: Security gates and software installed

May 1, 2017: Testing of circulation functions complete

July 1, 2017: Library opens

Ongoing: Tag and encode all new materials, replace nonworking tags, and train new staff and patrons

CHARTER ELEMENT #8: COST ESTIMATES

It can be a challenge to provide cost estimates this early in the project. If you are lucky, there may be existing information you can use. Maybe you are fortunate enough to have a grant or a request for proposals (RFPs). Maybe there are contracts already in place. In Pete's case, his director has provided both with the grant budget. If you don't have that luxury, you may be able to estimate your budget using historical data from other projects. Finally, your finance department may be able to provide some guidance.

Pete is fortunate that the grant provides the cost estimates for this project, but he checks to make sure he can deliver what is outlined in the drafted charter within that budget. Pete compares the grant budget against project requirements and finds that training and signage are included along with hardware, software, and supplies. He quantifies the cost of staff time on the project and adds that to the cost estimate.

If you are pressured to provide cost estimates before you have enough information, you may never recover. If you find you don't have what you need to reasonably estimate costs at this stage, discuss the situation with the project sponsor.

SIGN-OFFS

Each charter needs a place for the sponsor to sign the document to authorize the project formally. I have made the mistake of not getting a sign-off because it seemed like a formality. Please don't make that mistake. There's something that happens when people sign off on parts of the project: it makes them accountable. The sponsor's signature confirms that you're in this together.

Pete feels silly asking the director to sign the charter, and he considers sending the document to her via e-mail and asking for her commitment. He realizes that would be a missed opportunity. Pete requests a meeting with the director and adds two signature lines to the charter: one for the sponsor and one for the project manager.

A NOTE ON SCOPE

The charter is the first step in defining the scope of the project. Scope is "the sum of the products, services, and results to be provided on a project."[6] Scope tells everyone what you're going to do on this project, and it clarifies what you are not going to do. It's like a picture frame—what is inside the frame will be part of this project, and what is outside the frame won't be part of this project, though it could be part of a future one.

The project isn't going to deliver everything that people want. We write a charter because there are limitations or constraints on what we can accomplish. We can't spend unlimited money on the project, so cost is a constraint. We can't spend unlimited time on the project, so the schedule is a constraint. And we can't complete a project with every feature and functionality our stakeholders might want, so the scope is a constraint.

We call the limitations on cost, schedule, and scope the "triple constraint." They are not the only project constraints, but they are the three biggest constraints. If you change one, you change the others. Add scope to the project, and you add to the cost and the schedule as well. Defining and managing scope is one of the most important things you can do increase your chance of success: finishing on time and within budget.

Scope cannot be defined in a single sentence. Major deliverables, assumptions, and constraints are elements of project scope. Much of what goes in the charter provides a preliminary definition of the project scope. In the next phase of the project—planning—a group will further define scope and make a plan for controlling it.

SPECIAL CONSIDERATIONS

Sometimes a vendor will supply the library with a project charter. That is the vendor's charter for their business. It was written with their business needs in mind. This document should not replace the library's project charter.

Occasionally a project manager joins the project after the charter has been written. In that case, he or she should double-check to make sure the document gives the project manager the authority to use organizational resources. If you are the project manager and it doesn't, follow up. Early in the process is the best time to clarify your role and ask for what you need.

If information needed for the charter is difficult to obtain or estimate, the charter can be brief. In that case, more will be defined during the planning process. The majority of project work is iterative—we learn as we go, and we respond to what we learn. It is possible to change the project charter because it is possible to change any project document. However, changes should be formalized and include a review of how the changes impact time, cost, scope, quality, risk, and resources. Changing the charter is always a last resort.

Creating the charter is not just a formality. The process of writing and signing the charter will pay back dividends later in the project. When you use formal processes, assumptions get challenged. The right people get informed and engaged. The project sponsor has the necessary information and formalizes his or her commitment. The charter allows the project manager to be proactive instead of reactive. When difficulties arise—and they will—the project manager can point to the charter and say, "Remember when we met and we chose to do X instead of Y?"

SUMMING UP

- ☐ Do yourself a favor—always have a project sponsor.
- ☐ The charter clarifies and quantifies the work of the project and provides formal authorization to move forward. Reviewing the

charter with your sponsor should be a face-to-face discussion if possible.

☐ Change is hard for people. The more you can work with your colleagues in the early stages of the project, the more likely they are to step up later.

NOTES

1. B. R., "Planning and Procrastination," *The Economist*, October 6, 2012, www .economist.com/blogs/schumpeter/2012/10/z-business-quotations.

2. Project Management Institute, *A Guide to the Project Management Body of Knowledge: PMBOK® Guide* (Newtown Square, PA: Project Management Institute, 2017).

3. This quote has been commonly attributed to Peter Drucker, but that has not been confirmed. See "Culture Eats Strategy for Breakfast," *Quote Investigator* (blog), May 23, 2017, https://quoteinvestigator .com/2017/05/23/culture-eats/#note-16119-4.

4. Project Management Institute, *Guide to the Project Management Body of Knowledge*.

5. Ibid.

6. Ibid.

6
Getting to Know Your Stakeholders

I LIKE TO SAY THAT THE BEST PART OF PROJECT MANAGEMENT IS collaborating with other people...and the worst part of project management is collaborating with other people. When I've been successful at implementing new programming, other librarians helped me brainstorm, promoted the event, and came up with creative solutions for future programs. If I did library instruction well, it was because I worked with the professor to find out what would be meaningful to the students at that phase in their research. Ultimately, if I was successful when managing a project, it was because of collaboration with others. Yet collaboration with others has also had me pulling my hair out on occasion.

I was managing a software implementation for about twenty school districts when I learned a valuable lesson about working with stakeholders. The software we were installing would be used daily throughout every school in the district by teachers, office staff, and administrators. In my mind, all school officials would consider this a top-priority project. One day before a project meeting, I was chatting with one of the school's superintendents. I mentioned a message that had gone out via e-mail. He said offhandedly, "Oh, I don't read those e-mails." I was speechless. I wondered how we could ever be successful if he wasn't willing to receive my communication. When I got over my astonishment, I realized there were things I could have done differently during initiating that could have avoided this surprise: I could have done a better job working with stakeholders. Stakeholders are the people who are invested in the project because it will positively or negatively impact them in some way.

IDENTIFY STAKEHOLDERS

Anyone working on the project is a stakeholder, and so are patrons, vendors, volunteers, and others who will be affected. You have to plan early and earnestly to include them and to use their talents in the best way.

During initiating, project managers identify stakeholders in a document called a stakeholder register, shown in Figure 6.1. The stakeholder register does a few helpful things. It ensures that you consider the full range of people who will be impacted by the project. It forces you to think about what individual stakeholders need to know and what you need from those stakeholders. It is also great for reference because it puts name and contact information in one place. I use the stakeholder register throughout any project.

There are many ways to identify stakeholders. The project charter usually identifies influential stakeholders including the project sponsor. If the project uses vendors, requests for proposals (RFPs), requests for quotes, and contracts, those typically contain clues and possibly some specific names.

You may need to interview experts working on the project to identify stakeholders. Consider scheduling a short meeting with the project sponsor and those who will work on the project to ask "who" questions: Who will benefit from this project? Who is affected? Who has authority? Who can make our project succeed or fail? Is there anyone who wants this project to fail? Asking these questions builds your knowledge of the individuals necessary for project success.

ANALYZE STAKEHOLDERS

Different project stakeholders will require different things from the project manager. Some stakeholders only need to be kept informed, while others need to be engaged regularly. After identifying stakeholders, the next step, analysis, includes an assessment of each stakeholder's interest and power and then their engagement.

Analyzing the interest and power of the stakeholder helps the project manager use resources wisely. If I had done this with the school superintendent who didn't read my e-mails, I would have discovered that he had high

NAME	ORGANIZATION/ DEPARTMENT	CONTACT INFORMATION	NOTES	INTEREST/ INFLUENCE	CURRENT ENGAGEMENT/ DESIRED ENGAGEMENT
Sample: Joe Smith	Superintendent Lake Schools	joesmith@lake. edu	Send budget updates; send all other e-mail to Office Mgr Lois Wilson	Low/high	Neutral/neutral

FIGURE 6.1
Stakeholder Register

power but low interest. I might have asked a trusted colleague who worked with this superintendent on previous projects for suggestions on how to communicate best with him. I would have known to keep any meetings with this superintendent quick and to simplify any updates. A different superintendent on the project might have had high power and high interest and may have wanted to attend more meetings and receive more in-depth updates. My mistake was in grouping all superintendents together to receive the same information.

A project manager must consider power, but that doesn't mean we ignore low-power stakeholders. These are often the people who are going to do much of the hands-on work of the project. Low-power stakeholders are often subject matter experts, and their input is critical to project success. They should be kept informed and invited to participate where their subject matter expertise is needed.

The second part of stakeholder analysis is to identify current engagement and desired engagement. There are five categories of engagement:

- **Resistant:** These stakeholders don't like the change that is coming. They might not understand the change, they could be worried about job security, or they might be fatigued from previous projects. Typically, we want to move these stakeholders to neutral. If they become supporters, that's even better.

- **Unaware:** These stakeholders need to know the goals and vision of the project. It's your job to inform them.
- **Neutral:** These stakeholders are aware of the project. Be cautious so that they don't become resistant. If they are high power and high interest, work to move them to supportive.
- **Supportive:** These stakeholders are cooperative. Find ways to involve them.
- **Leading:** These are your project champions. Leading is where high-power, high-influence stakeholders should be. Involve them in your successes so they can spread the word.

On a large project with many stakeholders in different organizations, analyzing power, interest, and engagement is critical. A library consortium project to upgrade the catalog might include staff at forty different libraries. When so many people are involved, the project manager may not be able to meet every stakeholder. The stakeholder register will be an important reference when you create the communication plan. On a small project involving staff the project manager likely already knows, the process will be quick but still necessary. Sometimes knowing stakeholders means that we make assumptions about what they want and need. The register is an opportunity to ask each person, "What do you want to know about this project?"

The high-power, low-interest superintendent who didn't read e-mails was the perfect candidate for that question—"What do you want to know about this project?" He shared that his school district was facing significant funding challenges. He wanted information on the project budget and needed to delegate the rest of the project work to his office manager. I made changes to his information on the stakeholder register and added a row for the office manager. The superintendent's current engagement was neutral. Given the challenges on his plate, I decided it was unrealistic to try to move him to supportive. His desired engagement was also neutral.

It can be embarrassing when an important stakeholder is not identified at the beginning of the project. On a project involving multiple organizations, this is probably going to happen. When it does, reach out honestly and quickly: "I just realized you weren't included in our first project meeting. That was an oversight. I apologize. I'd like to invite you to our weekly status meetings and make sure you get future communication about the project." Then add the individual to the stakeholder register.

The stakeholder register is confidential. Just as a manager has notes that will be used to write a performance review, the stakeholder analysis provides the project manager with information needed to strategize. Be sure to keep the register in a safe place. Make a mental note of highly personal stakeholder information rather than recording the details in writing.

Once the charter has been written and signed by the sponsor and stakeholders have been identified and analyzed, the initiating phase is complete. The documents from initiating will become the building blocks for planning the project.

SUMMING UP

☐ You need stakeholder knowledge and skills to improve processes, manage risk, and get the work done.

☐ Ask your stakeholders how they would like to be involved with the project.

☐ Update your stakeholder register throughout the project.

7
The Planning Team

THE PROJECT CHARTER HAS COMMITTED RESOURCES TO THE project and established the sponsor. You know who your stakeholders are and understand their needs and expectations for involvement. Now it's time to create the project plan. In planning, you decide how you will accomplish the project. The planning phase of project management has more steps to complete than any of the other four phases. Don't be discouraged by the number of steps. If you have a small project, you can condense the steps into a few meetings.

The two documents created during the initiating phases are used throughout project planning: the project charter and the stakeholder register. Expert judgment and facilitation techniques are the tools you will use to develop the plan. Finally, because project work does not happen in a vacuum, you will consider environmental factors and organizational assets.

THE PLANNING TEAM

In initiating, you worked closely with the project sponsor and (hopefully) engaged a few colleagues as well. Now it's time to gather a formal team of people who can help you plan the project. This is your planning team. The *planning team* is different than the *project team*. The planning team includes experts who may not take part in the actual project work, while the project team is the group of people who will do the work outlined in the plan.

Sometimes your planning team is selected for you—for instance, when members are appointed to a committee. If you have the opportunity to choose your team members, invest time selecting the right people for the project. The charter outlined the work to be done, so by now you should have some ideas about the expertise you'll need.

The stakeholder register is a list of potential planning team members. Take a look at the register. Who has a lot of responsibility? Who has both interest and influence? Who do you want to engage? Those criteria may help you narrow the field.

Ensure that the planning team includes some of the people who will do the work of the project. These members will be part of the planning team and the project team. The learning that occurs during planning will be leveraged during project execution. Also, planning together will increase support for the project. People become invested in doing work that they helped plan. If the planning team and the project team are separate, there will almost certainly be pushback later.

In addition to expertise, consider the teamwork skills of potential members. Sound judgment and the ability to adapt are indications that a staff member may be a good collaborator. People who are respected by others make excellent project advocates—and you can always use an advocate.

Finally, consider diversity and inclusion when selecting a planning team. A diverse group may spend more time getting to consensus, but the time is well spent. The benefits of diversity include access to more knowledge, better decision-making, and increased stakeholder satisfaction.

You may have to negotiate to get the team members you want to plan the project. Be ready to make a case for the importance of the project, the need for a team member's skills and abilities, and the benefits for the individual and the department.

HOST A KICKOFF MEETING

In a football game, kickoff gets the team together on the field and starts a drive. Now that you have your project planning team confirmed, host a kickoff meeting. The kickoff meeting assembles the team and focuses on what's driving this project: your purpose and objectives. Kickoff is your chance to start the team off on the right foot.

A face-to-face meeting is ideal. If attendees are not located in the same place, a virtual conference is better than no meeting. Kickoff is your official announcement that the project has started. Your charter contains most of the information you'll share at the meeting. You will share the big picture, starting with why the library is doing this project right now. You are not just trying to deliver a new product or service on time and within budget. Explain how the project fits in with the strategic goals of the library. Review scope at a high level to help attendees understand what you'll create—and what isn't included. Give a brief description of project roles and their associated responsibilities. Reviewing both scope and roles now sets up clear expectations. Leave time for questions from the group and end your kickoff meeting by identifying the next steps.

Your kickoff meeting must include the planning team, and it usually includes the project team and stakeholders as well. You want to get everyone on the same page, so you will typically invite everyone to this high-level meeting. In some cases, when the project isn't defined clearly, you might choose to host the planning team only and then hold your official kickoff after project planning is complete.

The kickoff is also an opportunity to model the ethical values of responsibility, respect, fairness, and honesty. Show responsibility and respect for the team by preparing for this meeting and having an agenda with a purpose. Demonstrate fairness by allowing all team members the opportunity to speak and ask questions. Communicate transparently to establish honesty. These behaviors will become the foundation of your project.

AGILE PRACTICE
Self-Organizing Teams

Knowledge workers have to manage themselves.
They have to have autonomy.
—Rick Wartzman, "What Peter Drucker Knew about 2020"

One of the twelve principles of Agile is that "the best...designs emerge from self-organizing teams."[1] Agile works best on projects where scope will change rapidly and the team needs to respond quickly. If you are interested in empowering the planning team to be self-organizing instead of manager led, ask the following questions:

- Does this team embrace the purpose of the project?
- Will team members take responsibility for their work?
- Do the members trust and respect each other?
- Is this team cognitively diverse? Do members have different styles and experiences?

If the answer to all of these questions is yes, you may be able to let the group design their activities for project planning. In this situation, you will act as a servant leader, providing resources, documenting decisions, and lifting up issues the team cannot solve on its own. The team will define and schedule the work that needs to be completed. You'll still help with the overall project direction. If you think your team could successfully self-organize, use the kickoff meeting to confirm that the group wants to work together in this manner.

SUMMING UP

- ☐ If you get to choose your planning team, consider expertise, engagement, collaboration, and diversity as you select candidates.
- ☐ Ensure that your planning team includes some of the people who will do the work later.
- ☐ Use the kickoff meeting to establish why the project matters.

NOTE

1. Kent Beck et al., "Principles behind the Agile Manifesto," Manifesto for Agile Software Development, 2001, http://agilemanifesto.org/principles .html.

8
Planning Your Deliverable

Thirty years ago my older brother, who was ten years old at the time, was trying to get a report written on birds that he'd had three months to write, which was due the next day. We were out at our family cabin in Bolinas, and he was at the kitchen table close to tears, surrounded by binder paper and pencils and unopened books about birds, immobilized by the hugeness of the task ahead. Then my father sat down beside him put his arm around my brother's shoulder, and said, "Bird by bird, buddy. Just take it bird by bird."

—Anne Lamott, *Bird by Bird: Some Instructions on Writing and Life*

NOW THAT YOU HAVE YOUR PLANNING TEAM ASSEMBLED, you're ready to start creating a written project plan. The process begins by planning what the deliverable should be and how it should work (requirements) and what will and won't be included (scope).

PLAN THE REQUIREMENTS

Patrons often ask the reference question they think librarians can answer rather than the question they want answered.[1] When I get a reference question, I don't typically run to the stacks and start pulling out books. I take time to interview the patron. I've sometimes asked, "If I could find you the perfect piece of information, what would that be?" This question asks the patron to precisely specify what he or she requires.

The project manager guides the team in capturing what the project requires. Part of planning is to define what the thing (service, product, etc.) should do and how you will build it. Remember that preliminary requirements are in the charter. Those requirements may have been identified by an individual or a small team. It's time for the whole planning team to consider project needs in detail.

In 2014, 37 percent of all organizations reported inaccurate requirements as the primary reason for project failure.[2] Imagine a new group study room that is beautifully designed and outfitted with the latest digital media tech but sits without signage in an area not visible to users. It doesn't matter how great the space is if nobody can find it. Defining *visibility* and including that in the project plan as a requirement is a necessary step. Requirements are so vital that they are in the definition of project management: project management is the "application of knowledge, skills, tools, and techniques to project activities to meet the project *requirements*."[3]

Nobody wants to be surprised by critical requirements exposed at the end of the project—not the project manager and not the customer. A project that doesn't meet customer requirements is an unsuccessful project. If a library catalog vendor sells you a product that won't allow you to catalog media, you are going to be frustrated and angry. The ability to catalog different formats is a critical requirement. Even if you didn't specify this requirement, you still have a product you can't use. Invest time and energy in discovering, recording, reviewing, and getting approvals for requirements.

AN ASIDE: SPECS

In information technology, sometimes people use the word *specs*, or *specifications*. Specs are slightly different than requirements. Specifications are how the work will be done. There may be many different ways to do the work that could meet the project requirements.

DISCOVER REQUIREMENTS

Now that we know what the requirements are and why they are essential, how do we get them? There are three steps:

1. Discover.
2. Record and review.
3. Obtain approvals.

In discovery, the goal is to "seek first to understand."[4] There are many ways to get stakeholders thinking about requirements, and it's up to the project manager to determine which tools will work best. Techniques for discovery include reviewing existing documents, observation, one-on-one interviews, focus groups, and surveys.

Begin with less invasive techniques. Review organizational assets like training manuals, written reports, and e-mails to establish a basic understanding of the current state and the desired state. Observation is another technique to use early in the process to build knowledge. Study end users doing their jobs to learn the current workflow and identify opportunities for improvement.

Next, talk with stakeholders. Every stakeholder is a possible source of information for this stage of planning. Your project team, the sponsor, and vendors can all make meaningful contributions to requirements gathering. By involving all types of stakeholders, you reduce the risk of discovering a critical requirement near the end of the project.

End users are an especially important source of requirements. They will use whatever you are developing, and they are experts on what they want the product or service to do. End users do the work, they know what they want and need, and they can help you discover hidden project requirements.

Schedule one-on-one interviews with end users. Use the stakeholder register to identify potential interviewees. Don't limit yourself to interviewing only project supporters. Neutral and resistant stakeholders will help you uncover possible efficiencies and problems with existing systems. For a complex project, make a chart to document current workflows and ask end users to identify what's wrong in your chart. Use follow-up statements like "Help me understand why this step is necessary." Find out their daily, weekly, monthly, and yearly tasks.

Surveys are an excellent companion to one-on-one interviews. You may have received feedback from interviews that needs follow-up to see if what you learned is representative of the group. Surveys gather quantitative, as well as qualitative, data and they can get quick answers to pressing questions. Surveys are also helpful when people are geographically dispersed. If you need to follow up on survey responses, ask respondents to give their name and contact information.

Confidential and anonymous surveys are helpful when working on a politically sensitive topic. With a confidential survey, identifying data *could* be linked back to the individual respondent. An anonymous survey uses a generic link to the survey and does not collect any demographic data. If there is a lack of trust between employees and those in leadership roles, anonymous surveys may get you more honest responses, but you won't be able to group respondents in any way.

Focus groups are helpful after you've built your base of knowledge. A focus group is different than a meeting because it centers on a guided discussion on a defined topic—in this case, project requirements. Focus groups are designed to be maximally interactive. Participants talk to each other and can piggyback on ideas. This face-to-face, two-way, and real-time communication allows the group to go beyond discussion and make decisions about requirements. A MITRE Corporation guide states, "Joint (users, developers, integrators, systems engineering) requirements gathering sessions are frequently one of the most powerful techniques for eliciting requirements."[5] Because focus groups are so dynamic, it can be challenging to capture all that is said with notes alone. You may want to create video or audio recordings for reference.

One more way to elicit user requirements is to use prototyping. Prototypes create a model of what the project will produce. Prototypes work well for software and building projects. A prototype removes ambiguity and can result in more accurate requirements. When we renovated a library where I worked, we built a beautiful circulation desk. When we moved back into the library, we realized that there was no drop box for returns. At that point, there was no easy fix. The desk was constructed in a way that the ideal position for the drop box could not be accessed. The subject matter experts, the library staff, probably would have added the drop box to their specifications had they looked at a scale model of the desk. In general, responses will be richer when people can see the thing than when they have to imagine the thing.

RECORD AND REVIEW REQUIREMENTS

As soon as possible after discovering requirements, work with the notes and audio and video recordings to capture what was learned. Do this immediately after the event if possible when the information is fresh in your mind. Unedited notes become less useful as time passes.

Document all requirements in a spreadsheet (see Figure 8.1). Write requirements from the user's point of view whenever possible.

Next, check to see if each item meets the test of good requirements: requirements must be measurable and tied to the project objectives. Use the scope document from the charter to ensure that requirements "fit" within this project's boundaries. If you identify a requirement that is essential but doesn't fit within the scope defined by the charter, you may need to adjust your scope. Fortunately, revisiting scope is the very next step after defining requirements

REQUIREMENT	IS IT MEASURABLE?	IS IT TIED TO OBJECTIVES?	GENERATED BY WHOM?
Sample: I can see a library staff member when I walk in the front doors. (Note: This is from the user's point of view.)	Yes: Measure distance from door to reference desk and build prototype to ensure no visual obstacles.	Yes: Library redesign will be user-focused. Public service desks will have line of sight for greater safety.	Lois Smith

FIGURE 8.1
Requirements Template

in project planning. For those requirements that aren't measurable or tied to objectives, follow up with stakeholders using the contact information from the stakeholder register. Review the requirement together and identify ways to measure it.

If there are a large number of requirements, you will need to prioritize the list. Ranking is one method. When I worked in software development, we ranked requirements by how many users would benefit and how critical the requirement was to the proper functioning of the system. You can do this in a face-to-face meeting or use an online survey.

When requirements have been drafted, send them out along with any rankings for review. Schedule a meeting with the entire planning team and the project sponsor to review and assign responsibility for each requirement. It's possible that the meeting will reveal that some requirements in the draft need work, and that's a good outcome at this stage in the process. Use the meeting to resolve any issues.

This process takes time and effort, but it saves time and rework later in the project. It can eliminate a lot of questioning of decisions as well as costly last-minute changes. Taking time to plan requirements increases the chance that your project will fulfill the purpose and objectives you identified in your charter. When you have documented and ranked requirements to the satisfaction of the planning team, you are ready to obtain approvals.

OBTAIN APPROVALS FOR REQUIREMENTS

If the planning team has met to define and review requirements, why are formal approvals needed? Getting approval for project requirements is part of managing expectations. It's important for everyone to be clear on what it means for the project to be complete. As in the case of the charter, getting approval for requirements creates shared responsibility for project outcomes. Approvals also help you if your sponsor or a project leader leaves the project. The project manager will have documented, approved requirements to share with the new leadership.

Approach the process of getting approvals as a collaboration. Take the opportunity to make sure expectations between staff and administration match. Those conversations will build trust between those doing the work and those who will evaluate the outcome. For a smaller project, you may choose to delay requirements approval and do it at the same time as scope approval, the next step in project planning.

DETERMINING SCOPE

The requirements we just identified are used as we determine the scope of the project. In chapter 5, I said that scope is "the sum of the products, services, and results to be provided on a project."[6] The charter contains high-level information about scope. Now it's time to revisit scope to define it in more detail.

There are two types of scope: product scope and project scope. *Product scope* includes the features the end product should have—for instance, a new library should have restrooms. *Project scope* is the work required to produce the project's deliverable. It's all the work we do to complete the project. For instance, building a new library will require architectural plans, so those schematics are part of the project scope. Typically when the project is complete, only the product scope will be visible to users; patrons will see the bathrooms but not the blueprints. Project planning focuses on the work the team will do to create the project, so we are defining project scope.

Negotiating scope is one of the toughest challenges a project manager faces. There are many stakeholders, each with his or her own needs and desires. Time and cost constraints ensure that no one will get everything they want. Imagine renovating an academic library. Balancing the competing needs and wants of students, staff, faculty, and administration is a formidable task. As the popular saying goes, "You can't make everyone happy. You are not pizza."

The process for defining scope is the same as the process used to define requirements:

1. Discover.
2. Record and review.
3. Obtain approvals.

DISCOVER SCOPE

The planning team begins discovery with a review of the project requirements and the scope outlined in the charter. Earlier, I said scope is like a picture frame for the project. The requirements just identified have to fit within the frame. Compare the two. If there is a mismatch between requirements and scope, the team must address it now.

Project managers invest time to define the scope in detail because they want to prevent scope creep later in the project. Scope creep happens when work gets added to the project that was not included in the project plan. Scope creep has been called "kitchen sink syndrome," and it is one of the primary reasons that projects fail.

The same techniques used to discover requirements are used again: observation, one-on-one interviews, focus groups, and surveys. Record the information collected to review with the planning team. Meet with the team and work to gain consensus on project scope. Defining scope well helps manage stakeholder expectations later. Everyone on the team should agree on the scope.

RECORD AND REVIEW SCOPE

The planning team may need to list exclusions to the project to prevent scope creep. Exclusions are things that are outside the project scope. Pete's RFID project specifically excluded the local history collection. He added that exclusion to prevent confusion and to manage stakeholder expectations. Imagine if Pete's project didn't list that exclusion. Midway through the project, the head of local history might demand to know when the project team will start tagging his materials. Listing exclusions helps the project manager remain in a proactive rather than reactive position. What you exclude from this project could be part of a future project.

The project must balance and prioritize the needs of stakeholders to satisfy as many as possible and obtain a sign-off from those in authority.

OBTAIN APPROVALS FOR SCOPE

Obtain approvals from key stakeholders as well as the project sponsor by having them sign off on the scope definition. For smaller projects, you may get sign-offs for both requirements and scope at this time.

If getting a physical signature isn't possible at your library, make sure your project sponsor is at the review meeting. Get verbal agreement on the scope at the meeting, and document that in the meeting notes.

SUMMING UP

- ☐ Define the scope so you have a realistic documented summary of what you can accomplish with your resources for this project.
- ☐ Talking about what you can do with your current resources and what you can't do without more resources will ensure you aren't left "holding the bag" at the end of an unsuccessful project. Managing scope equals managing expectations.

NOTES

1. Robert S. Taylor, "Question-Negotiation and Information-Seeking in Libraries," *College & Research Libraries* 29, no. 3 (1968): 182, doi:10.21236/ad0659468.
2. Project Management Institute, "The High Cost of Low Performance," *PMI's Pulse of the Profession*, February 2014, www.pmi.org/-/media/pmi/documents/public/pdf/learning/thought-leadership/pulse/pulse-of-the-profession-2014.pdf.
3. Project Management Institute, *A Guide to the Project Management Body of Knowledge: PMBOK® Guide* (Newtown Square, PA: Project Management Institute, 2017).
4. Stephen R. Covey, *The 7 Habits of Highly Effective People* (Provo, UT: Franklin Covey, 1998).
5. MITRE Corporation, "Eliciting, Collecting, and Developing Requirements," March 3, 2016, www.mitre.org/publications/systems-engineering-guide/se-lifecycle-building-blocks/requirements-engineering/eliciting-collecting-and-developing-requirements.
6. Project Management Institute, *Guide to the Project Management Body of Knowledge*.

9
Planning for Risk

IMAGINE BEING PART OF THE PROJECT TEAM THAT WAS selected to build a new set of locks for the Panama Canal. Now imagine finding out that the planning team's winning bid was a billion dollars less than your closest competition. Your employer budgeted 25 percent less for steel and 75 percent less for concrete. That actually happened with the Panama Canal expansion project. Analysts studying the construction of the new locks noted, "There is little room in the budget for execution errors or significant inefficiencies. This is a high-risk situation."[1] By the end of the project, the canal's safety was under dispute, it was more than two years late, and cost overruns were $3.4 billion—more than the cost of the entire project.

Risk is "an event or condition that, if it occurs, has a positive or negative effect on one or more project objectives."[2] Planning for risk is another crucial step in project planning. The team may be able to mitigate or avoid some risks with good planning. Risk planning reminds me of going to a restaurant with a toddler—plan for the worst and hope for the best.

There are three steps for risk planning: identify, analyze, and plan responses. This risk assessment will affect the rest of project planning, including scheduling and budgeting.

IDENTIFY RISK

The question "Is there anything that could cause our project to be unsuccessful?" can help the planning team start identifying project risks. It's possible that you've already heard concerns about the project from the library staff. Subject matter experts are often quick to spot risks, and their ability to predict issues is an asset.

Begin with the risks listed in the charter, and brainstorm additional risks together. List as many risks as possible without judgment. Ask the planning team, "What are the risks that would impact time, cost, and scope?" Environmental factors like government mandates and legal issues are another source of possible risk to review. Do natural disasters like hurricanes, fires, or earthquakes pose any risk to the project? Ask the team if there are any risks to worker safety. In the next step, you will analyze each item, but brainstorming is necessary to first get ideas on paper.

There are many sources of risk in any project, and the planning team can get overwhelmed pretty quickly. By creating a comprehensive list of risks, the team is now collectively responsible for analyzing and planning for them. Risk management is everyone's job.

Check out this example. Remember Pete's RFID project? In the charter, three risks were identified:

1. If a staff member resigns, is out sick, is unable to do the work, or is significantly slower than his or her peers, the timeline may be negatively impacted.
2. If tags are not correctly encoded, staff will have to troubleshoot them at checkout, and that will result in no savings in time or even worse—it may take more time than the old system.
3. If patrons do not use the new self-checkout system, there will be no savings in time.

During planning, the team brainstorms additional risks, including the following:

4. The vendor could be late delivering equipment.
5. The vendor could be delayed with installation.
6. Construction in the building could make staff unable to access collections to do tagging and encoding.
7. Customer service for existing library operations could suffer because staff are less available.

In addition, Pete's planning team identifies a positive risk:

8. If circulation increases, there may not be enough self-check stations to handle the traffic at peak use times.

ANALYZE RISK

After risks are identified, the planning team moves to analyzing each risk. Risks vary by how likely they are to occur and the impact they could have on the project. Weigh each risk using the following formula: Impact × Probability = Actual Risk.

Let's look at the risks identified by Pete's team above and give each a score. (In this case, we are estimating rather than measuring risk. There are more precise methods, but they require expertise that is not available in most libraries.) We will use a scale of 1 to 5. A 5 is a worst-case scenario, and a 1 is minimal impact. Probability works the same, with a 5 very likely to happen at some point and 1 very unlikely. Since our scale is 1 to 5, the highest possible number would be 5 × 5, or 25. That's a risk that is a worst-case scenario and very likely to happen. The lowest is 1 × 1, or 1, a small impact that is very unlikely to happen.

1. Staff member gets sick or resigns: 2 × 1 = 2
2. Staff makes errors tagging and encoding: 4 × 3 = 12
3. Patrons don't utilize the new system: 4 × 1 = 4
4. Vendor is late on delivery: 4 × 2 = 8
5. Vendor is late on installation: 4 × 2 = 8
6. Patrons can't access the collection: 4 × 2 = 8
7. Customer service suffers: 3 × 1 = 3
8. Not enough equipment is available during busy periods: 2 × 1 = 2

Risks #1–7 would negatively impact the project. The planning team should create a contingency plan for each item identified, focusing their efforts on higher numbers. Based on these numbers, project manager Pete probably needs to have a risk strategy for staff making errors during tagging and encoding. Pete knows that some library staff are change averse and some are not technologically savvy, so he will plan for that possibility.

Risk #8 is a positive risk. Remember that a positive risk is an opportunity. For positive risks, strategize how to exploit or enhance them.

PLAN RISK RESPONSES

There are four strategies for managing negative risk on a project:

- accept
- avoid
- reduce
- transfer

Accepting the risk might be a strategy for a low-impact, low-likelihood risk. For staff missing work due to illness, the project manager may feel he or she can accept that risk. Pete might have a contingency plan such as asking staff to cover for a colleague who is out sick. With all staff trained on tagging and encoding, this is a workable contingency plan.

For the high-impact, high-probability risk of "staff makes errors," the planning team should not simply accept the risk. It also can't avoid the risk because they need existing staff to do the work. Transferring the risk would mean moving the risk to a third party, like buying insurance against the risk. The library is not going to buy insurance against staff errors, so the team isn't able to transfer it. The team will use the strategy of reducing the risk. Each staff member will be assessed after training to make sure he or she understands how to do the work. Specific staff will be assigned to the most challenging parts of the work. The team will plan to sample 5 percent of the work that each staff member performs to ensure that it is being done correctly. All of these efforts will reduce the risk.

For positive risk, the planning team also has four possible strategies:

- exploit
- share
- enhance
- accept

Pete's planning team determined it is unlikely that circulation will increase to the point that there are not enough self-checkout stations. It also decided the impact of the risk would be small. The team accepts the risk, knowing that staff can manually check out books if needed during peak use times. For each possible risk, the project manager documents the risk and the planned responses. Figure 9.1 is a sample template for these notes.

It takes time to identify, assess, and plan to manage risks. Why wouldn't a project manager just add days to the schedule or add money to the budget to cover risks? This kind of padding could allow the project manager to under promise and over deliver. Resist the urge. Padding is a sign of poor project management because it hides possible risk. Instead, do the contingency planning and document and communicate risk to key stakeholders. That's good project management.

RISK	SCORE	RESPONSE	ASSIGNED TO WHOM?
Staff make errors tagging and encoding.	12	Staff will complete quiz after training. Those scoring lower than 90 percent receive retraining.	Louella Humphry

FIGURE 9.1
Risk Management Plan

SUMMING UP

- ☐ Don't just worry about what could go wrong on the project—talk about it and plan for it.
- ☐ Subject matter experts can be helpful predictors of risk. Be sure to include them in your discussion.
- ☐ Padding the budget or the schedule hides risk; instead, be transparent and proactive.

NOTES

1. Walt Bogdanich, Jacqueline Williams, and Ana Graciela Méndez, "The New Panama Canal: A Risky Bet," *New York Times*, June 22, 2016, www.nytimes.com/interactive/2016/06/22/world/americas/panama-canal.html.

2. Project Management Institute, *A Guide to the Project Management Body of Knowledge: PMBOK® Guide* (Newtown Square, PA: Project Management Institute, 2017).

10
Schedule Planning

I love deadlines. I like the whooshing sound they
make as they fly by.

—Douglas Adams, *The Salmon of Doubt: Hitchhiking the Galaxy One Last Time*

WITH PROJECT REQUIREMENTS, SCOPE, AND RISK ADDRESSED, it's time to start on the part of planning that feels active—breaking down the work into activities and creating a schedule. The first step in the process is creating the work breakdown structure (WBS).

CREATE THE WORK BREAKDOWN STRUCTURE

The WBS is one of my favorite project management tools. The formal definition of a work breakdown structure is "a hierarchical decomposition of the total scope of work to be carried out by the project team to accomplish the project objectives and create the required deliverables."[1] It's the scope of the project organized into manageable deliverables. The WBS is a chart that shows your deliverables and the significant steps you will take to get there.

Let's look at a simple WBS for Pete's RFID project, shown in Figure 10.1.

How did Pete's planning team develop this WBS? They used their requirements and scope and met to break down the work into manageable chunks.

There are two guidelines the planning team used to create the WBS. The first guideline is to break down the work into three levels of detail. The second guideline is called the 8/80 rule: each work package (the items at the lowest level of the WBS) should take no less than eight and no more than eighty hours to complete. That is, each work package should take between one day and two weeks to complete.

There are several ways groups can work together to build a WBS. Pete chose to meet face-to-face with his planning team. He was concerned that some members would dominate the discussion, so he started with an activity that required everyone to participate. He gave each participant five blank sticky notes and asked them to independently write down five work packages necessary to complete the project. When all participants had their notes filled out, they put them on a whiteboard. The team could see areas of agreement right away. They used the rest of their meeting time to discuss the remainder of the work packages and to come to an agreement on those.

When the WBS is complete, the team moves to planning the project schedule.

FORECASTING YOUR SCHEDULE

Expert judgment is needed to create a schedule. If the planning team doesn't have expertise on all of the work packages, call in other people to help. Help might come from a subject matter expert from your organization, a consultant, or an experienced member of the vendor's team. Having knowledgeable people planning the schedule will improve your accuracy.

The steps for creating a schedule are the following:

1. Define activities.
2. Sequence activities.
3. Estimate durations.
4. Create schedule.

DEFINE ACTIVITIES

Before you can create a schedule, you need pieces of work that can be assigned to people. Those portions of work are called activities, and they come from

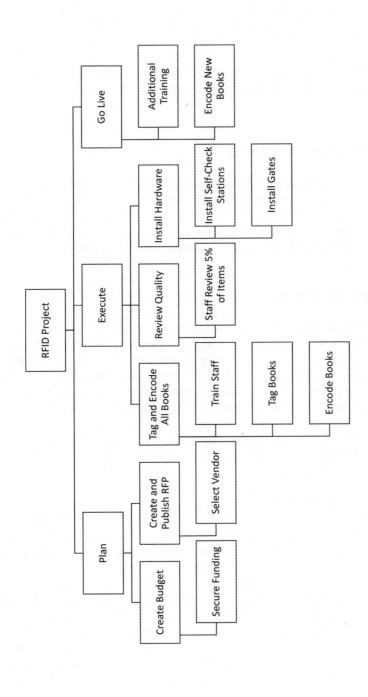

FIGURE 10.1

Sample Work Breakdown Structure

breaking down (or decomposing) the work packages in the WBS. One work package may have several activities required to complete it.

For Pete's RFID project, the WBS has a work package that reads "Install Gates." Pete knows that holes must be drilled in the floor for the gates. Drilling holes is an activity, part of the "Install Gates" work package. Drilling holes must be assigned to someone in facilities, and it needs to be part of the project schedule.

Agile Practice: Roll with It

If you can't decompose all of the work packages because you don't have enough information at this stage, you can begin by decomposing only the work packages that are near the beginning of the project. You will come back to this process later when you have more information. Working in phases this way is known as rolling wave planning. It's adaptive rather than predictive.

Confirm Resources

Before the planning team moves to sequencing activities, the project manager should review the activities identified and the resource needs of each. Now is a good time to confirm resources, starting with the people who are needed to do the work. Consider vacations, holidays, and training that impact staff availability. If staff are not 100 percent dedicated to the project (and they usually aren't), do they have the time to do the work required for this project? Also, think about the resources you need that are not human, including equipment, materials, workspace, and money. Be mindful of these constraints as you work on the schedule.

SEQUENCE ACTIVITIES

To identify the sequence of activities, ask the planning team, "In what order does the work occur?" Also, consider whether tasks must be done in a particular order or if that is simply a preference.

When building a library, you must pour the concrete foundation before you can frame the building. The sequence of activities is mandatory. It might be your preference to drywall the public areas before staff areas, so that sequence is discretionary. Finally, there may be an external agency that determines the order of the work. If you need wiring approved by the city before drywall can be hung, that's an external dependency. Knowing whether work is being done in a particular order because it is mandatory, discretionary, or an external dependency tells you if it's possible to make changes to the sequence of the work. The template in Figure 10.2 shows the data points for sequence activity planning.

Relationships between activities will determine the sequence of activities. You don't want to have a bottleneck in your project where work grinds to a halt. On Pete's RFID project, staff must be trained before they can begin tagging and encoding books. Training is called a "predecessor" activity, and tagging and encoding are "successor" activities.

There are also lags and leads in the project schedule. A lag adds time between activities. If there is a three-day break for the holidays, that is a lag. A lead decreases the time between two activities. In Pete's project, books must have a tag put in them before they can be encoded. Putting tags in all books will take three weeks. If Pete begins encoding the books that do have tags before the entire collection has been tagged, that's a lead.

ESTIMATE DURATIONS

Next, durations are estimated for each activity. The best estimates come from experience. Whenever possible, the person who will do the work estimates the work.

When you estimate at the activity level, you are using "bottom-up estimating." We provide estimates for each piece of work, and those estimates get added.

How would you get the estimate for the piece of work? The person who is going to do the work might use previous activities as the basis. They take that and add or subtract based on how this project is different. That's analogous

TASK ID	TASK	PREDECESSOR	WORK HOURS	DURATION	START DATE	END DATE

FIGURE 10.2
Sequence Activities

estimation. If you know how much time an individual unit of work takes, and you know how many individual units are in this project, you can multiply those two numbers. That's parametric estimation. Parametric estimating works if you have good data from the past that can be used in a reliable formula or model.

If you are unsure about durations, there are a few formulas that might help. I like three-point estimation:

$$(Optimistic + 4 (Most Likely) + Pessimistic) / 6$$

I think I can get training staff done in three days optimistically. In the past, it has taken a full week because of vacations and illness, so the "most likely" is five work days. And pessimistically, it could take two weeks—ten work days.

$$(3 + 4 (5) + 10) / 6 = 5.5$$

Round up your result to six days. Do this for every activity.

CREATE SCHEDULE

Now that you have activities sequenced and durations estimated, as well as an understanding of project dependencies, you are ready to create a schedule. Be realistic. Make sure the schedule can be accomplished with the resources you have.

Make a note of key dates and deadlines that are project milestones. Highlight those on the schedule. Milestones function like small goals and give the project team the opportunity to celebrate an accomplishment. They also serve as an early warning system—if a milestone is not met, the project manager must determine why and plan corrective action.

When you analyzed risk, you didn't add extra time to the schedule for surprises. If you used the formula for duration with optimistic, most likely, and pessimistic estimates and you worked with the group of people who will do the work to come up with those numbers, you should not need to pad your durations.

Your software is only as good as what you tell it. It takes the information you provide and creates the schedule. You still have to understand and enter the work, the relationships, and the estimates.

SUMMING UP

- ☐ Work with your experts to agree on a reasonable schedule.
- ☐ If you don't have enough information to complete a full schedule, start with what you know and alert your sponsor that more information is needed.
- ☐ While project management software can be helpful with scheduling, it is only as good as what you tell it. You must understand and enter the work, the relationships, and the estimates.

NOTE

1. Project Management Institute, *A Guide to the Project Management Body of Knowledge: PMBOK® Guide* (Newtown Square, PA: Project Management Institute, 2017).

11
Planning Who Will Do the Work

EARLIER, THE PROJECT MANAGER DECIDED WHO WAS NEEDED
to *plan* the work. Now that the WBS is complete, the planning team can
analyze who will be needed to *do* the work.

CLARIFY ROLES

On many library projects, project team members don't report to the project
manager. They report to a functional manager, such as the head of IT. That
means the project manager has considerable responsibility but little authority. Informal authority is one reason that it is crucial to discuss roles openly.
People who work on the project need to understand what they will be doing,
what others will do, and what they can expect from the project manager.
Reviewing roles is an opportunity to prevent role confusion and another
chance to manage expectations.

The following list is an example of how you might clarify project roles:

- The sponsor champions the project and removes obstacles.

- The project manager ensures that the project achieves its objectives on time and within budget.
- Planning team members provide expert judgment to define project requirements and scope.
- Project team members actively work on project deliverables.
- Stakeholders respond to requests for information and read project communication.

Just as we listed exclusions in the project scope, it may be helpful to list exclusions in the project roles:

- The project manager is accountable for creating the WBS but is not responsible for completing project activities.

Some planning teams use a chart to clarify roles and responsibilities called a responsibility assignment matrix or RAM (see Figure 11.1). It is also sometimes called a RACI chart because it lists who is responsible, accountable, consulted, and informed (RACI) for each task.

Responsible: This is the person who does the work.
Accountable: This is the person who makes sure the work gets done correctly. Those responsible for doing an activity are accountable to this person.
Consulted: This is someone who doesn't do the work but can help inform the work. Often these people are subject matter experts and stakeholders.
Informed: This is the person who will receive the finished activity or who needs to stay informed.

There are two rules when creating the RAM:

1. every activity needs a person accountable and at least one person responsible and
2. there should only be one person accountable for each activity.

To create a RAM, add each project activity to the first column in the order of completion. Identify project roles and list them across the top of the chart. Ideally, complete the rest of the cells with the planning team. If that's not possible, complete and then share the chart with the rest of the team and request feedback. The planning team must agree on roles before beginning work on the project.

The RAM can also be helpful during project execution. If you add columns for due date and status, the chart can be used to keep everyone informed of progress.

ACTIVITY/ DELIVERABLE	SPONSOR	PROJECT MANAGER	PROJECT TEAM	STAKEHOLDER
	Name:	Name:	Name:	Name:
Ex: Create project budget.	A	R	C	I

FIGURE 11.1
Responsibility Assignment Matrix

COMMUNICATION PLANNING

The team has planned to manage scope, risk, and the schedule and is now planning to manage human resources. Part of managing people is managing communication. If you provide good communication with your planning and project teams, team members will support you through rough times. If you've left them in the dark, later you may find yourself on your own. Communication is especially important if you are an informal project manager. You won't have formal authority over the project team, but you can use communication to support and engage team members. The majority of a project manager's time is spent communicating. A communication plan is needed to ensure people have the right information at the right time.

Have you ever wondered how a simple message you shared got you into trouble? I have, and it's frustrating. You've probably heard people say, "The single biggest problem in communication is the illusion that it has taken place." When I learned about the number of communication channels on a project, I started to understand why and how this happens.

Take a look at your stakeholder register. How many stakeholders do you have? The number of communication channels for a project is determined using the number of stakeholders. The formula is

$$n(n-1)/2$$

where n is the number of stakeholders. If your project has ten stakeholders, then you have

$$10(10-1)/2$$

for a total of forty-five communication channels. Add one more stakeholder, and the number becomes fifty-five communication channels. Communicating to report, delegate, motivate, and lead is a complicated job because of the number of communication channels.

One out of five projects is unsuccessful due to project communication issues. What's more, organizations that are not effective with communication are likely to experience repeated failure: "Among those organizations considered highly effective communicators, 80 percent of projects meet original goals, versus only 52 percent at their minimally effective counterparts."[1]

Part of this problem is the Dunning-Kruger effect, which tells us that people are likely to overestimate their abilities in areas where they are unskilled. The skills needed to recognize problems with communication are the same skills required to be good at communication. While 62 percent of business owners and 60 percent of sponsors think they are communicating effectively, only 43 percent of project managers agree.[2]

Communication methods can be broken into three types: interactive, push, and pull.

1. Interactive communication includes face-to-face conversations and is multidirectional. It is the best way to ensure understanding because it allows for immediate follow-up questions.
2. Push communication is sent to recipients, but there is not a way to make sure it was received and understood. Push communication methods include letters, memos, and e-mail.

3. Pull recipients must access the communication. Examples include online courses, Internet sites, and surveys.

All types of communication are good when used appropriately. Push communication would be used to invite stakeholders to a kickoff meeting. Pull communication is used when a project team member goes to the shared drive to access a document. Interactive communication is appropriate for a performance review.

A communication plan allows you to be proactive, planning for the information stakeholders will need and when they will need it. It also ensures that misconceptions and rumors don't take hold. To create a communication plan, start with your stakeholder register. Using the template shown in Figure 11.2, make sure each stakeholder is assigned to at least one group.

TRAINING AND TEAM BUILDING

There are two more human resources (HR) plans you may need for your project. If your project team members require training, you will need to create a training plan. The plan outlines the training resources required, including staff attendance and funds, and it serves as a formal request for those resources. Additionally, a team building plan can help you create cooperation and collaboration.

Team building should get people out of their silos, working together on a common goal. Team building activities can be as simple as eating lunch together or as elaborate as a multiday retreat. Here are four inexpensive project team building activities:

1. Provide professional development—attending training and workshops together.
2. Include icebreakers at the beginning of meetings.
3. Volunteer together.
4. Take a project-related field trip.

In your team building plan, you might consider how you plan to recognize and reward exceptional performance. Even if project team members don't report to you, you can let them know you appreciate their work. Here are thirteen ideas:

1. Say thank you.
2. Bring in breakfast or lunch.
3. Pay for valuable training.
4. Offer time off, like leaving an hour early.
5. Write a letter to their supervisor or HR.

WHAT	WHO			WHEN	HOW	WHY
Type	**Who Sends?**	**Who Receives?**	**Who Authorizes?**	**Schedule/Frequency**	**Format/Method**	**Purpose**
Kickoff meeting	Project manager	All teams	Sponsor	July 15 at 2:30 p.m. / one time	Meeting/invitation sent via e-mail	Communicate plans, celebrate
Weekly status updates	Project manager	All stakeholders	N/A	Friday mornings / weekly	PDF/sent via e-mail	Share data on progress
Annual report	Foundation staff	All stakeholders	Director	Annually	Document/sent via mail and e-mail	Celebrate accomplishments, inform donors and public

FIGURE 11.2

Communication Plan by Event

6. Pay for an association membership.
7. Recommend them for a raise or a work assignment.
8. Offer small prizes.
9. Throw a party.
10. Create opportunities to work on things they enjoy.
11. Reassign a responsibility the staff member doesn't enjoy.
12. Create a reserved parking spot.
13. Host a casual dress day.

There is one more team building activity to plan: celebrations. When the project team meets a milestone or finishes the project, a celebration is in order. Plan to celebrate achievements together throughout the project by assigning specific dates on your calendar. Later, when you are busy, they will be there to remind you that it is important to pause and have a little fun.

Take the time to build healthy teams, and you will improve communication and increase collaboration to raise your chances of project success.

SUMMING UP

☐ Managing expectations is a big job. Define roles so that your project team members know who is doing what.

☐ The number of communication channels on a project can be enormous. Plan communication so that people stay informed.

☐ The more work you have to do on your project, the more you need a plan for recognition and rewards. Plan now to keep team members engaged throughout the project.

NOTES

1. Project Management Institute, "Communication: The Message Is Clear," *PMI White Paper*, December 2013, www.pmi.org/-/media/pmi/documents/public/pdf/white-papers/communications.pdf.

2. Project Management Institute, "The High Cost of Low Performance," *PMI's Pulse of the Profession*, May 2013, www.pmi.org/-/media/pmi/documents/public/pdf/learning/thought-leadership/pulse/the-essential-role-of-communications.pdf.

12
Costs and Budget Planning

W E ARE NEARING THE END OF THE PLANNING PROCESS. IT'S time to think about how much money you will spend, how much quality you need, and how much change you can handle.

HOW MUCH MONEY: ESTIMATE COSTS AND CREATE A BUDGET

If you are an unofficial project manager, you may not get the opportunity to craft your budget. It may be given to you. You still need to understand the process of creating a budget so that you can be fiscally responsible. If the budget passed down to you is not sufficient for the project, you'll need to know what to ask for from your project sponsor. The more specific and detailed you can be when you make a request, the better chance you have of getting what you requested. It is difficult to take responsibility for a budget you don't understand, so ask questions about anything that is unclear.

A budget is the approved estimate for the project. If you are charged with developing the project budget, all of the planning up to this point will give you the tools you need. Knowing the work down to the activity level provides information about the resources required to complete the project. The more detail, the better the estimates you can create. If you have deconstructed your work packages to the activity level and identified the resources and time needed for each work package, you can create a budget within the scope of your project.

If you are new to budgeting or new to the organization, work with someone who has done this before. If you can't get one-on-one assistance, ask for examples from previous projects. Historical data, including costs on past projects, will be useful. You may also have contracts or RFP responses with specific costs listed.

To draft your budget, you will want to think about both direct and indirect costs. Direct costs can be attributed to your specific project. They might include software, computer purchases, and staff time. Indirect costs are harder to calculate for the project. They include things like heating and lighting the building and depreciation. You may not need to include indirect costs in your project budget. Also, consider both fixed and variable costs as you estimate. Some costs will be fixed and stay the same no matter how long your project lasts. Purchasing software could be a fixed cost. Variable costs change depending on how long the project takes. If you hire temporary help to move books for a renovation knowing it will take between two and four weeks, that's a variable cost. The cost goes up with time.

You may have to estimate some costs on your project. In areas where you make estimates, document your basis of estimates. The basis of estimates is a document that details how you arrived at each number in your estimates. Later, you may not remember how you came up with these numbers. If something changes or your boss asks for more detail, you'll want this document to remind you what you were thinking. If you have good notes, you can respond to requests and issues with confidence.

You may be concerned about cost overruns. What do you do in the middle of the project if your estimates were too low? Remember the reasons that you didn't pad your timeline? Don't pad your budget either. If you do, you hide the cost of the project. Your library deserves to know the actual cost of the project. Additionally, "extra" money has a way of getting spent—you might use up that pad when it isn't truly needed.

Instead, use a contingency or a management reserve. Contingency reserves are specifically for work packages. Here's an example: You need temporary workers to move books, and you aren't sure how long it will take. You think it will take two weeks and you know that cost, but it might take four weeks. You could budget a contingency reserve to address this variable cost. If you've never done this work package, it's not surprising that you have some uncertainty. Add a line for the contingency. When the work is done, if you didn't need the contingency, the funds are released and not used. The project isn't hiding funds.

A management reserve is another way to handle the unexpected. It's not tied to a work package; instead, a management reserve is for the entire project. You might put aside an extra 5 percent to cover things not covered by contingency reserves. Make this a separate item from the rest of your budget. Your budget without the management reserve is still the project budget; the reserve is a separate item only to be used with specific permission.

Confirm the accuracy of your draft budget before you request approval. Think of a few respected colleagues and ask them to review your draft budget. All budgets must be approved. Once approved, your budget (without any management reserves) is your baseline budget. It's the yardstick you use as you track spending. Later, you will report your actual costs, compare them to the baseline, and report any differences and why they occurred.

HOW MUCH QUALITY

What is quality? It's the degree to which your product or service fulfills requirements. If a shelver puts books on shelves in the wrong call number order, you have a quality problem. If you build a library and the foundation crumbles during the first year, you have a quality problem. During the planning stage, the planning team defines quality and decides what to measure and report. The goal is to identify problems and respond quickly.

The first step in planning for quality is defining it. Quality standards come from three places: project requirements, industry standards, and your library's standards. For example, the Library of Congress provides industry standards on image quality for digitization projects. Additionally, stakeholders and subject matter experts can help define quality.

Once you have a definition of quality, the planning team can set quality targets. Document selected targets in the project plan. Targets tell workers on the project what to measure during execution. You can't control what you don't measure.

When you have targets selected, determine how data will be reported. How do workers communicate the data, who reviews it, and how does it get reported? There is a common saying among statisticians: "Data is like garbage. You'd better know what you are going to do with it before you collect it."

On Pete's RFID project, he plans to have a staff member check the quality of tagging and encoding of books. One staff member is selected to follow the tagging and encoding project team, and she will sample three books per shelf. If an error is found in any of the three books, all books on the shelf will be checked. Data are collected for each shelf, and Pete checks the chart each morning. Error data are included in the weekly report, which is sent to the project team and the sponsor.

HOW MUCH CHANGE

You've worked hard to define project requirements and scope, to develop a schedule and budget, and to analyze and plan for human resources and risk. For the rest of this project, you're going to manage change to all of those areas of your plan. Requests for changes come about for a variety of reasons, including stakeholders, newly discovered requirements, natural disasters, and even federal mandates.

Many times, customers change their minds about what they want during their projects. Imagine you are the head of IT and are implementing a new library catalog. You've already been through initiating and planning, and you are nearly finished configuring the system. In a meeting, the circulation manager says she needs the system to flag patrons with $5 or more in fines. Then the collection manager comes back from a conference where he watched a demo of a competitor's software, and he wants to automatically get an e-mail when a new MARC record is added to the catalog. Finally, the head of documents sends an e-mail saying she must have a customized cataloging portal.

These are all reasonable requests, but they weren't discovered during requirements gathering. The problem is that they are not on the schedule or in the budget. Adding them will mean more time and possibly more cost. What should the project manager do? If you've planned for this, you'll have a process to handle it.

Your change control plan should include a process for evaluating, approving or denying, and communicating changes to the project team. Start with who will receive requests. Large projects typically have a change control board—a group of people, including the sponsor, who review and respond to change requests. You may not need a board for your project, but it would be wise to give responsibility for approving changes to your sponsor or another person above the project manager.

The change request log (see Figure 12.1) ensures you get basic information for each request, and it's a vehicle to communicate and analyze the request with your change control group.

Having a change control procedure gives you a standard way to evaluate costs and benefits before proceeding. Sometimes there is another way to meet the need without changing the scope. The experts on your project team may be able to suggest alternatives.

Project Name _____

Requested By _____ Date _____

Describe Change Request

Reasons for the Change

Impact of Making This Change:

On the Schedule	
On the Budget	
On Human Resources	
On Quality	

_____ Approved _____ Denied

By (Name) _____ Date _____

Signature _____

FIGURE 12.1
Change Request Log Template

Change requests have a reason and should be handled promptly. There are times when there is a compelling need to make a change. If a change request is approved, the project manager may need to change the budget and schedule. Be sure to do so, as that can be the difference between project success and failure.

AN ASIDE: INHERITED PROJECTS

We've been discussing planning a project in the ideal circumstances where the project manager is involved from project initiation. Sometimes a project manager inherits a project. If this happens to you, expect to take over a project that has problems. Plan for the worst and hope for the best.

If you inherit a project, start by requesting project documents. Sit down with the project sponsor and let them know you're going to need information. If you're taking on a project with problems, you need to be able to ask difficult questions. Is there a charter or project plan? Those will help you identify expectations. If there was no charter or project plan, are there any contracts? Has a schedule been created? Ask if priorities have changed since the project kicked off. Find out what communication has been sent and to whom. Analyze what you learn to determine if this project is feasible.

If you have concerns but agree to be the project manager, you could create a restructuring plan to be signed by your project sponsor. It can be abbreviated if time is limited, as it often is in inherited projects. Finally, ask library leadership to communicate their support for your appointment as project manager. Their backing provides you a solid foundation for beginning your work with a team that may be reticent to accept a new manager.

Once the team has been informed, plan to meet with them right away. Focus on reviewing scope, status reports, and risk management. You'll also need to invest time and energy in building the morale of the project team. They may have difficulty trusting you. If that's the case, exhibiting the values from the project management code of ethics is going to be even more critical. Find opportunities to demonstrate responsibility, respect, fairness, and honesty with your project team.

PLANS EVOLVE

In the planning phase, you and the team made the best decisions possible with existing information. Some aspects of the plan won't be finalized until you have more information. Plan to revisit previous decisions and discussions throughout the project life cycle. There is good news: This means that the plan doesn't have to be perfect.

SUMMING UP

- ☐ Document what you were thinking for any estimates you make during the budgeting process.
- ☐ Have a plan to manage change.
- ☐ If you take on a project already in progress, ask for the resources you need to be successful.

13
Executing

WITH THE PROJECT MANAGEMENT PLAN COMPLETE, IT'S TIME to take a deep breath and start "doing" the project. You've planned your work; now you work your plan. Executing means doing the work in the plan to create the product as specified.

Katie was in charge of developing the public library's first online summer reading program. Her team had a fantastic time planning the program. Katie was excited to show off their work at the monthly all-staff meeting. The presentation would be the first step in executing the project plan.

Katie's meeting would begin with an overview of the program, and then her planning team member from IT, Joe, would demonstrate the live site. Katie planned to practice the presentation with Joe the day before the meeting. That morning, though, a workman accidentally cut a cable, and the library's Internet was down. Joe had to cancel at the last minute to deal with the crisis. Katie reminded herself of Joe's technical strengths and professionalism and figured that things would go smoothly.

Things didn't go smoothly. Katie got to the meeting room early to turn on the projector and pull up the site. She couldn't get the summer reading program website to load. Staff arrived for the meeting, and Joe improvised by showing mockups of the site and explaining how patrons would interact with each page. Some of the library staff were sympathetic, but others expressed frustration. If the site didn't work now with no traffic, what made Katie and Joe think it would work all summer long with thousands of users? Next, a staff member brought up an unrelated IT problem from several years ago. Katie saw where the meeting was headed and thanked everyone for their time. She let them know that she would be following up soon. She ended the meeting.

Executing is when the rubber hits the road. The project becomes a reality, and people are doing things in new or different ways. Conflict is almost inevitable. During executing, conflict is often about schedules, priorities, and resources.

DEFINE CONFLICT

We all know the difficulties of conflict: conflict creates challenges that we have to address with time, energy, and occasionally money. It adds stress. However, conflict also has some benefits. As people discuss the conflict, more information gets revealed. This information might not have come to light if there were immediate consensus. It can help teams identify defects in the plan and then address them. Conflict can uncover attitudes and opinions of team members, which can help the project manager strategize how to manage the project team. Finally, conflict sometimes illuminates who is in charge of the project. It helps the group understand authority.

When conflicts arise, there are five conflict management techniques the project manager can use:

1. **Withdrawing:** Retreat or postpone a decision.
2. **Smoothing:** Focus on agreements and ignore differences of opinion.
3. **Forcing:** Push one viewpoint.
4. **Compromising:** Find solutions to satisfy both parties.
5. **Collaborating:** Openly discuss differences and find consensus.

There is no one-size-fits-all approach to conflict management. Usually collaborating is the best solution, but there are situations when one of the other techniques may be the best choice.

Withdrawing gives the problem the opportunity to grow and spread, but it can be useful when the project manager needs information and time before addressing an issue. Smoothing happens when the project manager concedes to the other party. Smoothing can be helpful when goodwill is essential, but it is a poor long-term strategy because passivity from the project manager can deprive the team of leadership. Forcing happens when the project manager ignores the needs of individuals and creates a win-lose situation. It is the equivalent of saying, "It's my way or the highway." Forcing should be used sparingly—only when stakes are high, relationships are not important, and time is of the essence. Compromising allows both parties to get something they need and allows the project to move forward. Collaborating requires both time and trust but can result in a win-win solution. The people involved meet face-to-face to discuss the issue and find a solution that satisfies the concerns of both parties. If the conditions are right for collaboration, this is the preferred technique because it leads to learning and higher satisfaction.

The people best able to address the conflict are the people involved in the conflict. The project manager could help facilitate a resolution if he or she has authority over those involved in the dispute. If not, it may be more appropriate for the sponsor or the person's manager to address the issue. There is one exception to this rule: if the conflict is a result of unethical behavior or illegal activity, then the project manager must go beyond the people involved to make a report.

Katie withdrew from her meeting because she was not prepared to address the technical problem with the site at that moment. She ended her meeting as quickly as possible when she saw conflict spiraling out of control. Using this technique, she gained a little time to think and to problem solve. Katie was willing to lose the battle to win the war.

In the executing phase, the project manager manages the project team, leads communication, and produces deliverables. Katie must focus on all three to recover from the meeting and return to her plan of execution. Katie knows that accountability is the most important thing she can model right now because it's what she needs in return from everyone else on the project. Katie should follow up with her planning team first and then with the rest of the library staff.

MANAGE THE TEAM

During executing, you choose any additional project team members needed to do the work and then implement your plans for team building and recognition.

Expanding Your Team

Have you heard the one about the chicken who suggests to her friend Pig that they start a restaurant? Pig says, "I'm interested. What would we call it?" Chicken thinks for a moment and then cackles, "Ham and Eggs!" Pig replies, "Oh, no—no, thank you. I'd be committed. You'd only be involved."

People new to the project may not be as committed to the work. They haven't been with you through the planning process. Make sure they are clear on why this project is important to your organization.

If you're using library staff to do the work, take a look at your pool. Experienced and talented staff may already have a full plate. In some organizations, the same people get assigned to tough jobs repeatedly. The reward for hard work is more hard work. Good people leave organizations because of this. If that's been the case in your organization, it's time to develop other staff members. Consider whether you can use the project to give a less experienced worker an opportunity. That would be a good choice for a less risky part of the project.

You need people who are available to do the work. Talk with supervisors to see if you can get any job responsibilities suspended while the person is working on the project.

Building Your Team

In the previous phase, you developed a team building plan. Get those activities scheduled now. If you didn't create a team building plan, assess the project team now. Are the members cooperating and collaborating? If not, it isn't too late to make plans.

Projects face challenges because people face challenges. Learning new skills, changing processes and roles, and working with new people are all uncomfortable experiences. You can help project team members work through these experiences in several ways:

1. Model professional growth by learning alongside your project team. Attend training and workshops together if possible. Acknowledge your mistakes.
2. Connect your team members to a network. Introduce them to important contacts, make use of professional associations, and plan a networking lunch or event.
3. Provide frequent feedback. Notice what's going well and what could have gone better.

Recognize and Reward Your Team

Recognize staff for their work as soon and as often as you are able. Use the plan you made in the previous phase. If you didn't make one then, there are still plenty of easy and inexpensive things you can do for your project team. The cost of recognition is typically your attention and a few minutes of your time. If you're not sure of the best way to reward your team members, ask them.

Now that you're doing the project, you will observe staff taking the initiative and working hard. Recognition should be specific. Mention the behavior you observed and why you appreciate it. In addition to the ways you planned to recognize staff, give verbal thanks to individuals and teams in your meetings.

Manage Communication

In the planning phase, the team invested time in planning project communication. In executing, the project manager puts the plan into motion. Communication during project execution includes sending and receiving messages, reporting on performance, managing engagement and expectations, and hosting stakeholder meetings.

E-mail is a convenient way to communicate, but it doesn't build strong relationships. Your recipients can't see your facial expression or hear the tone of your voice, and you can't see theirs in response to your message. Asking multipart questions via e-mail doesn't usually work well. When you have the opportunity to talk with stakeholders face-to-face, make the most of it. Temporarily let go of your agenda and the point you want to make. This is far easier said than done. However, if you listen only for a pause in the conversation to reply, you limit what you learn from the other person. Mistakes in projects happen because of assumptions, and the only way to get past your assumptions is to listen more than you speak.

After Katie's disappointing summer reading program presentation, her first task was to meet with her project team. Katie asked her team to come prepared to talk about what went wrong from a technical perspective. She acknowledged it was uncomfortable learning in front of the entire library staff, but they did gain useful information at the meeting: the site needed work. Katie asked the group to review the facts of what happened and then discuss the impact. Katie acted as note taker so that she could ask clarifying questions but not lead the discussion. Next, the team created action items to address the issues. Katie made sure each item was assigned to a team member. With this in place, Katie could plan her communication to stakeholders.

Katie was not in the proactive place she wanted to be for project communication at launch. She did have everyone's attention, though. She used this to demonstrate her accountability and commitment to the project. When the site had been fixed, Katie and Joe met with each public service agency to demonstrate. The small groups worked well—staff members were reassured to see a working website, and they had the opportunity to ask questions.

After hosting individual agency meetings, Katie followed up with an e-mail survey to ask each attendee what worked well and what could be improved. She asked staff to give their names on the survey so she could follow up if needed. This feedback allowed Katie to improve the deliverable—the final summer reading website.

AGILE PRACTICE: THE DAILY MEETING

Agile practices utilize a daily project status meeting called a scrum. This status meeting is held every morning in the same place at the same time and lasts no more than fifteen minutes. Team members working on the project report on their progress, and others can attend as listeners. There are three questions answered by each team member:

1. What did you do yesterday?
2. What will you do today?
3. Are there any obstacles in your way?

The project manager is responsible for addressing question three by removing obstacles or finding someone who can remove them. This typically happens outside the fifteen-minute meeting.

Why is the scrum-style meeting valuable? It has several benefits. It is an efficient communication method. It pushes team members to be responsible for their work. It reveals problems early so they can be addressed. All three of these benefits are an answer to the problem of "social loafing." Social loafing happens when a person exerts less effort because they are part of a group. Usually, team members will step up their game because of the accountability built into the daily scrum. If that doesn't happen, the group will know early on and the project manager can do something about it.

One important takeaway from this Agile practice is to be consistent. The project status meeting happens regularly, not just when there is a problem. If you can't meet daily, meet weekly on the same day and at the same time each week. If your team members work in different buildings, plan a conference call instead of a face-to-face meeting. Keep the meeting as short as possible and resolve issues that were raised during the meeting afterward when possible.

DON'T SKIP THIS: THE PROJECT STATUS MEETING

A scrum meeting does not replace the need to report on scope, budget, and schedule to stakeholders outside the project team. Your sponsor should receive this information regularly. Establish a regular project status meeting.

This meeting is the most important thing you can do during executing to increase your chances of project success. If the project manager or a member of the team doesn't do the work that was planned, the project fails. Your project status meeting keeps everyone accountable and informed.

PRODUCE DELIVERABLES

During executing, deliverables are produced. It is satisfying to see the work of the project moving forward. Unfortunately, it's also the time when issues come to light. Issues are problems that weren't planned for but require action. While risks are things that might happen, issues are things that *are* happening.

Here are some examples of issues:

1. During a data conversion, you realize the data you planned to export out of your old system are of poor quality and must be cleaned.
2. During a building project, you see your brand-new library circulation desk and realize that there is a support brace exactly where the drop box should have been placed.
3. During an RFID project, you discover that your old security tags are on the same frequency as your new tags and interfere with the signal.

Issue logs are a way to track problems as they are discovered, to assign them to the right people, and to make sure they get resolved. Using an issue log is a way to move from blaming to assigning the problem to an owner to be resolved. Blame interferes with relationships and communication, while issue tracking places the focus on problem solving. Figure 13.1 shows an issue log template.

CELEBRATE

There's one more important thing that you need to do during executing. Celebrate accomplishments as you achieve them with the project team. It's easy to get busy doing things and to miss this step, but celebrating your successes will help you carry the group through the challenges of the project. On really tough projects, sometimes a strong relationship is the best tool you have to keep team members engaged. If you included celebrations in your team building plan, you're ready to implement those activities. If not, a celebration can be as simple as mentioning what is going well in your regular meeting and asking for a round of applause. Just as you remind the group why the project is important, remind the team that they are making progress.

ISSUE	RAISED BY	ON (DATE)	PRIORITY	ASSIGNED TO	TARGET RESOLUTION DATE	STATUS	ACTIONS	RESOLUTION
Ex: Data in name fields is inconsistent.	Amanda	January 1, 2018	High	Dirk	March 1, 2018	In progress	Writing script to clean up	

FIGURE 13.1

Issue Log

SUMMING UP

- ☐ Conflict may be inevitable, but you can choose how to respond.
- ☐ Hold regular project status meetings. Whether it's a daily scrum or a weekly meeting, consistency is critical.
- ☐ Use an issue log to track problems that arise during executing.

14
Monitoring and Controlling

"THEY DON'T DO WHAT YOU EXPECT; THEY DO WHAT YOU INSPECT."
This was my mother's advice to me when I complained that my children weren't doing their chores properly. I realized this is true of my behavior as well. When I know that someone else is paying attention, I do better work. When people depend on me, I do my best work. Being held accountable helps us all.

Monitoring and controlling are different than the other phases of the project because they happen throughout the entire project. Monitoring and controlling are integrated into the initiating, planning, executing, and closing processes. While PMI lists monitoring and controlling as a separate process group, some project management books do not. Understanding monitoring and controlling is critical when things don't go as planned.

The monitoring and controlling phase is focused on achieving the objectives of the project. In order to achieve project objectives, the triple constraints of cost, schedule, and scope must be monitored and controlled. You'll compare planned performance to actual performance. Monitoring and controlling involve tracking, reviewing, and regulating process and performance.

If you did a thorough job initiating and planning the project, then you've set yourself up for success with monitoring and controlling. Pete's RFID project is a good example of how tracking, review, and regulating process and performance happen during project execution. Staff placing RFID tags in books and those doing the encoding logged the call number of ranges they completed daily. The simple log was the tool for tracking. The log served several purposes: staff on the next shift would know where to begin their work, and Pete would have current information on project progress. Additionally, the log was used for quality checks outlined by the project plan. The assigned staff person would check the daily log for ranges completed the previous day and would sample a portion of those books. This review revealed that some staff were not placing the tags in the correct position inside books. Fortunately, sampling was done as soon as possible after the work, and the error was caught quickly before a lot of tags were wasted. While .07 cents per tag isn't a lot of money, it adds up quickly—150,000 tags cost more than $10,000. To improve performance, Pete hosted a five-minute retraining on tag placement, showing correct and incorrect examples. That solved the problem.

Another issue spotted by sampling was incorrect encoding. In one range, barcodes didn't match RFID tag numbers. Pete was alerted and got to work looking for the cause. He determined the issue was user error. The settings in the software were wrong. Pete changed the daily process of setting up computers to include a checklist. A small group reencoded all books from the previous day to correct the errors. As frustrating as the rework was, the sampling process functioned just as planned. It caught problems in quality that would have been more costly to fix later in the project. If the issues had not been identified during the project, they would have been found by users. Students would not have been able to successfully check out those books using the self-checkout. The students' perception would have been "this system doesn't work."

Pete caught errors in his project early because he had a plan for monitoring and controlling. Another way projects get in trouble is scope creep. Previously, I said that scope creep happens when additional work gets added to the project that wasn't in the plan. *Scope Creep* would be an excellent title for a horror movie for project managers. Part of monitoring and controlling your project is preventing scope creep when possible.

Remember Katie's online summer reading program project? She had so much success showing off the site to each department that she was asked to bring the adult summer reading program online as well. Katie was concerned that this change in scope would stretch project resources beyond capacity. Fortunately, the planning team for Katie's project had defined change control procedures. Katie took the request to the project sponsor, the library director, who rejected the change request for this project based on the short timeline. There just wasn't enough time to add more modules. Though adult reading wouldn't be part of that year's online offering, it could be a project in the future.

The change control process is the best defense you have against scope creep. Put all requests through your process, starting with a written change request. Your change control team will be familiar with your scope statement, project schedule, and deliverables. They will evaluate the impact of the change on the project. If the change control team approves the change, you'll change your project documents, including your budget and schedule.

OVER BUDGET, OVER TIME

What do you do when your project is over budget or late? Sometimes it's not anyone's fault that the project is at risk. For example, a natural disaster can make a project late. Whatever the reason, you must recover. The project manager must translate project data from information into knowledge. That knowledge is used to determine what action, if any, must be taken.

Start by gathering data and asking questions. What happened? Why did it happen? Who made the decision resulting in the overage? Follow up with that person. You must find out what is causing the project to be late or over budget and then halt that activity. Next, assess the impact with regard to scope, budget, and time. Call your project team together and ask for insights, alternatives, and recommendations. Notify your change control team and your sponsor. Share what you found—what happened, why, and how it will impact the project. Share recommendations from the project team and confer with the group on a decision. Inform others who may need to know, like vendors or specific stakeholders. Next, update the plan and then implement the changes.

SUMMING UP

- ☐ Mistakes happen. Monitor the project so you catch them early.
- ☐ Being over budget and late won't get better magically. Be honest about your project status.
- ☐ Your change control team is your secret weapon to protect the project from scope creep.

15
Closing

C LOSING IS THE MOST IGNORED OF THE PHASES OF PROJECT management. Sometimes the project fizzles out. Sometimes the project manager goes on to work on another project. At this stage of a project, the team might be eager to move on to something new. Everyone wants to wrap up, get paid, and move on.

I was working on a large data project using an expensive software package. After our initial implementation, the project manager wanted sign-offs and closure of the project. I felt we still had a lot of work to do together and knew we would continue to pay for services for at least a year, so I didn't understand why she was so keen to close our project. I see that differently now that I've studied project management. The deliverable was complete. Our future work together could be part of a new project with new objectives.

In closing, the project gets formally accepted as complete. Remember, the definition of a project states that it has a definite end. No matter what, the project gets closed rather than being allowed to linger. Closing is just as necessary as the rest of the phases, and without it, the project is not complete. Closing your project is not the end. The end comes after the project is closed.

Closing is your chance to polish your project and distinguish yourself as a finisher. Even an unsuccessful project gets closed. Skipping the closing phase increases risk, results in losses to the organization, and undermines your credibility. Figure 15.1 shows a closing checklist.

Six things need to happen during closing:

1. Obtain acceptance of deliverables.
2. Issue payments.
3. Document lessons learned.
4. Create, present, and submit a final report.
5. Reassign resources.
6. Celebrate!

ACCEPT DELIVERABLES

Confirm that all requirements have been met before you request a sign-off. Review your objectives, success criteria, and requirements. Check that all tasks in the WBS were completed. Ensure that all change requests were reviewed and approved change requests are complete. If all of that is done, you're ready to request sign-offs.

If issues prevent acceptance by your customers, negotiate a solution or settlement. You could use a punch list, as is done with construction projects. A punch list is a list of work that must be done to in order to meet project specifications. The deliverable is not accepted until the punch list is complete. Acceptance of the deliverables is one of those formal steps that is incredibly important.

PAY EVERYONE

If there were contracts or vendors, they must be closed out. You don't want to get an invoice three months later for work that you can't remember. When the work in any contract is confirmed as complete, make payments. This is also the time to compute the final costs of the project.

DOCUMENT LESSONS LEARNED

Seek feedback from your stakeholders. Find out how you did with your project management practices, and document your lessons learned for use on future

✓	**ACCEPT DELIVERABLES**
	Confirm all requirements have been met:
	Review objectives, success criteria, and the requirements listed in the charter. Were those met?
	Were all tasks in the WBS completed?
	Were all change requests completed?
	Review deliverables with sponsor.
	Schedule a review with the customer to obtain his or her sign-off.
	If there are issues, negotiate a solution.
✓	**PAY EVERYONE**
	Make final payments.
	Close procurements.
✓	**DOCUMENT LESSONS LEARNED**
	Do postproject evaluations:
	From team
	From customer
	Include process improvement.
✓	**CREATE AND DELIVER FINAL REPORT**
	Distribute report to sponsor, team members, and stakeholders.
	Archive important files (schedules, budgets, changes).
✓	**REASSIGN RESOURCES**
	Review team member performance.
	Write any letters to document new skills or kudos.
	Release or notify staff of new assignments. Release equipment.
✓	**CELEBRATE**
	Gather and share appreciation.

FIGURE 15.1

Closing Checklist

library projects. Evaluation is only done 20 to 30 percent of the time, and that's a significant missed opportunity. As Warren Buffett said, "In the business world, the rearview mirror is always clearer than the windshield."[1] You can solicit feedback by asking questions like the following:

- What did we do well?
- What could we have done better?
- Are you satisfied with the outcome of the project?

If you love this part of project work, you can do it each time a milestone is achieved—you don't have to wait until the end of the project. If it is the end of the project and you are short on time, create an online survey to collect feedback. Remember that "your most unhappy customers are your greatest source of learning."[2]

CREATE AND DELIVER FINAL REPORT

Write a final report, and, if possible, present it to the sponsor and project team. Include a project overview and list the original objectives. Include your final schedule and budget, and explain any variances. Include an overview of lessons learned and any outstanding action items. If the project was closed before completion, document the reasons and the status. Archive any project files with your final report.

REASSIGN RESOURCES

Your project team members get back to their regular jobs. If appropriate, send letters to human resources to document any new skills or appreciation for their work.

CELEBRATE

Have you ever had a project end with no formal recognition that it is over? Even though you celebrated your milestones as you achieved them during executing, it's important to end your project with a final celebration. Gather for a meal, bring in treats, or find a way to give a heartfelt thank you. This is your final opportunity for team building. You've probably heard the saying, "I've learned that people will forget what you said, people will forget what you did, but people will never forget how you made them feel."[3]

An Aside: Project Failure

*Failure is simply the opportunity to begin
again, this time more intelligently.*

—Henry Ford

So your project failed. I have heard more than once that the project manager is the person responsible for the success of the project. I have to disagree. The project manager is the person focused on the success of the project, but he or she is not the only person responsible for success or failure. Ninety-four percent of projects fail due to the systems and processes employed.[4] A project manager cannot singlehandedly change organizational systems and processes. "The project manager is *responsible* for many things, including leadership, but the sponsor is always ultimately *accountable* for the success of the project. It's the sponsor who must have the authority, skill, will and ability to enforce the project manager's direction, reallocate resources and resolve conflicts above the project manager's level of influence if projects are to succeed. If a project fails because of a shortage of human resources or a drop in funding from the organization, for example, pinning the fault on the project manager is a mistake."[5]

The American Management Association says that projects fail for four reasons:

1. The project was not clearly defined.
2. Plans were not developed with the team.
3. Stakeholders had unrealistic expectations of project management software capability.
4. The project manager or the team was mismanaged.[6]

If the only thing you can salvage out of the lost resources of time, money, and employee engagement is learning, you owe it to your library to learn. Document the reasons for failure in your report. Your honesty may help change the system and processes for the next project.

SUMMING UP

- ☐ Closing allows you to tie up any loose ends.
- ☐ Document what you learned, and archive your files for future reference.
- ☐ Thank your team members for their work.

NOTES

1. Catherine Taibi, "The 16 Best Things Warren Buffett Has Ever Said," *Huffington Post*, August 30, 2013, www.huffingtonpost.com/2013/08/30/warren-buffett-quotes_n_3842509.html.
2. Bill Gates, *Business at the Speed of Thought* (New York: Warner Books, 1999).
3. Richard Evans, *Richard Evans' Quote Book* (Salt Lake City, UT: Publishers Press, 1971).
4. William Edwards Deming, *Out of the Crisis* (Cambridge: MIT Press, 2000).
5. David Whitemyer, "The Blame Game," *PM Network* 27, no. 1 (January 2013): 62–65, www.pmi.org/learning/library/blame-game-project-failure-4021.
6. American Management Association, "Why Projects Fail," 2004, www.amanet.org/training/articles/why-projects-fail.aspx.

Afterword

*It's hard to imagine how you would go about
delivering a project without program and
project management discipline. Without a
consistent approach and clear milestones,
decision points and metrics to measure your
success, you're just flying by the seat of your pants.*[1]

ALA'S WEBSITE FOR THE CENTER FOR THE FUTURE OF LIBRAR-
ies includes a list of thirty trends that are relevant to libraries and librarianship.[2] From blockchain to gamification to the sharing economy, all of these
trends began as someone's crazy idea that became a project and then became
wildly successful.

Since I started working in libraries in the 1990s, budgets and staffing
have declined. At the same time, competition from other information sources
has risen. Interestingly, it was in the 1990s that I started to see articles and

books on project management in libraries, like Liz Maclachlan's 1996 book *Making Project Management Work for You*, part of the Successful LIS Professional series. I believe this is because my fellow library professionals are organized innovators, and project management is one means for creating and responding to trends and challenges in smart ways.

We are challenged to make wise investments with our resources, often doing new things with old processes and tools. Project management will not solve systematic problems within our institutions and our society, but it can be a framework for doing work differently. The meaningful part of project management is not creating charts or writing plans. It's the conversations, the transparency, the negotiation, and the collaborative problem solving that are required to create the right result.

If you apply the skills, tools, and techniques outlined in this book while practicing responsibility, respect, fairness, and honesty, you will have better project outcomes. Following every step in this book might make you a better project manager, but finding the right balance between process and people will make you a great project manager.

I believe the future of project management in libraries will be unofficial. Regardless of our titles, we will be required to manage projects in a rapidly changing landscape. We will see more digitization, more transformation, and more challenges. Now is a great time to implement some project management principles and find out what works for you.

NOTES

1. Project Management Institute, "The Value of Project Management," *PMI White Paper*, 2010, www.pmi.org/business-solutions/white-papers/value-project-management.
2. American Library Association, "Trends," August 8, 2014, www.ala.org/tools/future/trends.

Bibliography

Adams, Douglas. *The Salmon of Doubt: Hitchhiking the Galaxy One Last Time*. London: Pan, 2012.

American Library Association. "Professional Ethics." January 22, 2008. www.ala.org/tools/ethics.

American Library Association. "Trends." August 8, 2014. www.ala.org/tools/future/trends.

American Management Association. "Why Projects Fail." 2004. www.amanet.org/training/articles/why-projects-fail.aspx.

Andersen, Erika. "21 Quotes from Henry Ford on Business, Leadership and Life." *Forbes*, July 7, 2014. www.forbes.com/sites/erikaandersen/2013/05/31/21-quotes-from-henry-ford-on-business-leadership-and-life.

Bain & Company. "Busy CEOs Spend Nearly One Day Each Week Managing Communications, Two Days in Meetings." May 6, 2014. www.bain.com/about/press/press-releases/Busy-ceos-spend-nearly-one-day-each-week-managing-communications.aspx.

Beck, Kent, et al. "Principles behind the Agile Manifesto." Manifesto for Agile Software Development, 2001. http://agilemanifesto.org/principles.html.

Bogdanich, Walt, Jacqueline Williams, and Ana Graciela Méndez. "The New Panama Canal: A Risky Bet." *New York Times*, June 22, 2016. www.nytimes.com/ interactive/2016/06/22/world/americas/panama-canal.html.

B. R. "Planning and Procrastination." *The Economist*, October 6, 2012. www. economist.com/blogs/schumpeter/2012/10/z-business-quotations.

Connell, J. B. *Flying without a Helicopter*. Bloomington, IN: iUniverse, 2014. https:// books.google.com/books?id=skbYBQAAQBAJ.

Covey, Stephen R. *The 7 Habits of Highly Effective People*. Provo, UT: Franklin Covey, 1998.

Deming, William Edwards. *Out of the Crisis*. Cambridge, MA: MIT Press, 2000.

DuBrin, Andrew J. *Essentials of Management*. 9th ed. Mason, OH: South-Western / Thomson Learning, 2012.

Evans, Richard. *Richard Evans' Quote Book*. Salt Lake City, UT: Publishers Press, 1971.

Gates, Bill. *Business at the Speed of Thought*. New York: Warner Books, 1999.

Goleman, Daniel. *Working with Emotional Intelligence*. New York: Bantam Books, 2006.

Kinkus, Jane. "Project Management Skills: A Literature Review and Content Analysis of Librarian Position Announcements." *College and Research Libraries* 68, no. 4 (2007): 352–63. http://crl.acrl.org/index.php/crl/article/ download/15880/17326.

Lamott, Anne. *Bird by Bird: Some Instructions on Writing and Life*. Melbourne: Scribe, 2009.

MITRE Corporation. "Eliciting, Collecting, and Developing Requirements." March 3, 2016. www.mitre.org/publications/systems-engineering-guide/se-lifecycle- building-blocks/requirements-engineering/eliciting-collecting-and-developing- requirements.

Project Management Institute. "Code of Ethics and Professional Conduct." Last revised October 2006. www.pmi.org/-/media/pmi/documents/public/pdf/ ethics/pmi-code-of-ethics.pdf?sc_lang_temp=en.

Project Management Institute. "Communication: The Message Is Clear." *PMI White Paper*, December 2013. www.pmi.org/-/media/pmi/documents/public/pdf/ white-papers/communications.pdf.

Project Management Institute. "Ethical Decision-Making Framework." 2012. www. pmi.org/-/media/pmi/documents/public/pdf/ethics/ethical-decision-making- framework.pdf?sc_lang_temp=en.

Project Management Institute. *A Guide to the Project Management Body of Knowledge: PMBOK® Guide*. Newtown Square, PA: Project Management Institute, 2017.

Project Management Institute. "The High Cost of Low Performance." *PMI's Pulse of the Profession*, 2013. www.pmi.org/-/media/pmi/documents/public/pdf/learning/ thought-leadership/pulse/the-essential-role-of-communications.pdf.

Project Management Institute. "The High Cost of Low Performance." *PMI's Pulse of the Profession*, 2014. www.pmi.org/-/media/pmi/documents/public/pdf/learning/thought-leadership/pulse/pulse-of-the-profession-2014.pdf.

Project Management Institute. "The High Cost of Low Performance." *PMI's Pulse of the Profession*, 2016. www.pmi.org/-/media/pmi/documents/public/pdf/learning/thought-leadership/pulse/pulse-of-the-profession-2016.pdf.

Project Management Institute. "The Value of Project Management." *PMI White Paper*, 2010. www.pmi.org/business-solutions/white-papers/value-project-management.

Taibi, Catherine. "The 16 Best Things Warren Buffett Has Ever Said." *Huffington Post*, August 30, 2013. www.huffingtonpost.com/2013/08/30/warren-buffett-quotes_n_3842509.html.

Taylor, Robert S. "Question-Negotiation and Information-Seeking in Libraries." *College & Research Libraries* 29, no. 3 (1968): 178–94. doi:10.21236/ad0659468.

Tennant, Roy. "The Single Best Tech Skill Is Tenacity." The Digital Shift. Posted January 25, 2012. www.thedigitalshift.com/2012/01/roy-tennant-digital-libraries/the-single-best-tech-skill-is-tenacity/#_.

Wartzman, Rick. "What Peter Drucker Knew about 2020." *Harvard Business Review*, October 16, 2014. https://hbr.org/2014/10/what-peter-drucker-knew-about-2020.

Webber, Michael, and Larry Webber. *IT Governance: Policies and Procedures*. Alphen aan den Rijn, Netherlands: Wolters Kluwer Law & Business, 2016.

Whitemyer, David. "The Blame Game." *PM Network* 27, no. 1 (January 2013): 62–65. www.pmi.org/learning/library/blame-game-project-failure-4021.

Index